WinningAutocross Solo II Competition
the art and the science

Best of luck,
Rick Turner

Winning Autocross Solo II Competition

the art and the science

turner & miles

Copyright ©, 1977

All Rights Reserved

The text of this publication, or any part thereof, may not be reproduced or transmitted in any form or by any means, electronic or mechanical, including photocopying, recording, storage in an information retrieval system, or otherwise, without the prior written permission of the authors.

Library of Congress Catalog Number
77-87119

Printed in the United States of America

ISBN 0-932522-01-7

For further information concerning courses, programs and printed material please contact:

National Academy for Professional Driving, Inc.
Competition Division
2711 Cedar Springs
Dallas, Texas 75201
214/742-3471

Winning Autocross / Solo II Competition
The art and the science

Written by — *Richard H. Turner* / *J. B. Miles*
Type face used — *Megaron*
Typesetting and Production — *Zebra Graphics, Inc.*
Illustrations and Cover Design — *Athel Reed*
Production supervision by — *The Printer of Dallas, Inc.*
Printing and Bindery by — *Hicks Printing Company*

This book is dedicated to three outstanding people without whose efforts, assistance, and "dammit, write the thing," we would still be bench racing.

To Bob Brittain, the man who refired a detuned racer, kindled the flame of desire, and makes each day better,

Roger Eandi who knows which button to push, the words to say, and the short line up the hill in Oakland,

And Clarita Robertson, a beautiful lady who listened while others laughed, coaxed while others criticized, and acted while others watched,

We say thanks. The three of you make our lives easier, our dreams a reality, and tomorrow even brighter than today.

—Dick & J.B.

Contents

Foreword 8
Introduction 9
The Body 13
The Head 15
The Hands 18
The Feet 26
Shifting 34
Accelerating and Braking Forces 40
Basic Suspension Functions 43
Tires 48
Conditioned Reflex Autocrossing and
  the Closed Loop System 52
Trailing Accelerator, Trailing Brake,
  and Torque Lag 59
Types of Corners 65
Cornering and Tire Pressure Guidelines 73
Time Ranking 80
Reading a Racing Surface 83
Sideslipping and Emergency Brake Turns 87
Driving to the Store, or, How to Drive Your
  Easy Chair 92
Transient Response 94
Polar Moment 96
Hydroplaning and the Autocross Car 99
Critiquing Your Performance 102
Autocrossing on Paper 105
The NAPD Home Course 110
Driving Exercises 114
Tips 'n' Tricks 117
Common Mistakes 122
Dave Shelton 124
Glossary of Terms 125

Foreword

I met Dick Turner when **Autoweek** learned about his police driving school in Texas. Here was a story, we decided. I was sent immediately to the inferno that is Texas in July, to cover the police school, we thought. It developed that the better story was the autocross school.

Here was a virtual road course for autocrossers, who have learned to be satisfied with supermarket parking lots and obsolescent airstrips. More important, here was a driving school proprietor who stayed out on the course, teaching. With the temperature topping out at 109° in the humidity of an aquarium, this was impressive.

Most impressive was the improvement in my driving after two days at the school. I had been told by other **Autoweek** editors that I would return an autocross devotee. They were right. I had been told I would come back shocked at the extent of my previous ignorance about driving a car, and they were right about that, too.

Not long after I completed the school and the story appeared in **Autoweek,** I received a phone call from Turner. He had been mailed the galleys of a book he was writing about autocross driving techniques, with friend and former autocross pupil J. B. Miles. He asked if I would like to see the book. Willingly I accepted.

Of course it was the book you have in your hand. As I read the rough galley, I realized Turner and Miles had produced a volume which communicated many of the lessons I had learned during my two days in Texas.

Turner admits reading the book will not make a champion out of a beginner. It is my feeling, however, that it might make a winner out of a loser. Not every loser, necessarily; but any enthusiast who is making some or all of the mistakes common to most autocrossers, beginners as well as veterans, might be surprised at how often he or she finishes in the trophies with a little work and study.

I probably will never go back to Texas, unless Turner offers an advanced course at his facility. I will keep my copy of **Winning Autocross** at hand whenever I'm watching or participating in an autocross event, however. I always have been a believer in home study, and in postgraduate work. This book is the best way I know to go faster, without buying a turbocharger.

Charles L. Cannon
Associate Editor, **Autoweek**®

Introduction

Throughout history, man has been a competitive creature. As he learned to run, he raced other runners. Later, he learned how to ride a stronger, faster animal, and one man raced his animal against another's.

Then came the automobile. Almost as soon as the motor car was invented, some men were obsessed with making it go faster. Various types of measurement were devised to tell who had actually gone the fastest, farthest, or best. Man raced against man in machines designed for only one purpose, to go fast.

Later, man tried to go fast against a clock. Man against time is perhaps the ultimate form of motor sport. Qualification runs determine who will start in front at Indianapolis, LeMans, or Devil's Bowl. Special qualification engines are commonplace in NASCAR competition. Gumball tires were designed for one purpose: to go fast for a little while and qualify in front.

If such is the case, solo events—or autocrossing—must rank high on man's list of ultimate achievements. As with all forms of motor sport, there are two sides of the coin. Dirt trackers love physical contact with other cars. Formula one drivers love the combination of man, machine, track, and other cars and drivers to compete against. Drag racers prove their engineering ability against time, and another car. Solo drivers combine all of these elements. We decided it was time for someone to print the secrets of autocrossing, hoping to improve the state of the art even more.

Ask any driver the key to autocross victory, and sooner or

later in your conversation, a statement will be made about driving smoothly.

We'll examine what smoothness is, why it is necessary, and how to achieve a smooth driving habit.

We'll discuss such things as transient response, tractive forces, moments of intertia, cornering, shifting, accelerating, braking, and how to win trophies.

We obviously cannot teach you how to become an autocross champion by reading a book. We can, however, give you the keys to help improve your driving ability, and make your car less of a mystery to you. Only through constant practice, and unfailing discipline will you ever become a consistent winner. In our world, there is winning, then everything else. We'll give you moves to practice that produce winners.

This text is written to the advanced practitioner as well as for the beginner. It is our claim that winning in solo competition does not take years of working your way up through the ranks. In fact, one of our students, a female college student, started winning a week after completing school. She must like it, because she hasn't finished out of the trophies since!

If you are willing to dedicate your driving hours to constant improvement, you can practice correct moves on your way to the store, or sitting in your living room. Yes, you read it right, we said IN YOUR LIVING ROOM.

Why do we make such brash statements? In our opinion, driving is ninety percent mental, and only ten percent physical. Thus, ninety percent of what your goal is can be practiced anywhere your head is!

An average one minute solo event requires approximately seven hundred mental mini-decisions. This means over ten tiny inputs are happening every second. By comparison, only about sixty to seventy physical moves take place each minute, or approximately one per second. If you are making more than seventy physical moves per minute, you are probably wasting valuable time.

In solo competition, we can do only two things: Preserve time, or lose time. There is no such thing as gaining time, since a clock starts when we leave the first gate, and doesn't stop until we get to our final gate. Therefore, every mental or physical move we make is evaluated in terms of time. If we move at an optimum rate, we are preserving time. Anything else is costing time.

To boil this book down to the bottom line, we are going to show you how to spend less time getting from start to finish. When Mr. Webster defined time as "the period between two events, or during which something exists, happens, etc.," he probably did not realize that he was setting a stage for the most intense type of competition known to autosport.

We will deal in thousandths of a second. At sixty miles per hour, we are traveling 1.056 inches per one-thousandth of a second. Normal solo events are run at speeds averaging less than sixty miles per hour. This means we are traveling less than 1.056 inches per one-thousandth of a second. How many times have you seen a class run to less than one-one hundredth of a second for the top four or five places? Our friend, and student, Bill Dawson ran first in an event recently. Third place was only .017 seconds slower. The event was a high speed type, where the average speed was quite close to sixty miles per hour. This means the third place finisher was only 17 inches slower than Bill. While he's telling everybody how close he came, the first place trophy lives at Bill's house! This is what we are talking about.

As you read this book, then practice what you have read, watch out for other people. Don't allow yourself to become a SNIOP. A SNIOP is someone who is 'Subject to the Negative Influence of Other People.' When discussing what you have learned with someone who has not read the book, but is a self proclaimed expert, do not allow yourself to feel inferior because you sought help while they already know all the answers. If they are that sharp, you can buy a copy of their book some day.

Doesn't it stand to reason that your competitors would rather have you lose? If such is the case, how valid is their 'help' to begin with? Without flashing our credentials too strongly, accept one statement, what we have to offer has come from years of dedication, facts based on scientific research, and WINNING.

We are going to ask you to try moves that will feel foreign. Don't give up after three or four unsuccessful tries — only constant practice makes winners. If you want to win, read on. If you are trying to learn how to run second, take this critter back to the store, you have wasted your money. We don't know how to train you to run second!

Autocrossing is both an art and a science. Your car is based on science. How you drive it is based on science, with a touch of art thrown in. Yes, a true competitor is an artist.

The authors are scientists by training, and artists by choice. How and why they win will be revealed to you in this book.

Dick Turner has spent over twenty years figuring out why a car does what it does, how to make it do better, and how to teach someone else tricks of the sport. His credentials include a background in auto racing, a Ph.D. in concept design, and his current status as chairman of the board of directors of National Academy for Police Driving, Inc. in Dallas, Texas. In addition, Turner also holds a Doctor of Education degree, and a Doctor of Laws degree.

J. B. Miles was born and reared in Dallas, and has been involved in serious autocrossing for the past four years. Prior to that time, he was a motorcycle racer, having been a road racer for three years.

J. B. attended Arlington State, then Texas Tech University in Lubbock, Texas. In addition, he was involved with the Adjutant General School at Ft. Benjamin Harrison, a member of the U.S. Army pistol team, and a target bow shooter. He is currently a contractor, and he and Dick Turner share a love for racing, and the how's and why's of automotive perfection.

NAPD has revolutionized police driving, and the competition division has turned out some excellent autocross drivers. A sixteen hour intensive autocross course is offered by NAPD either at the home base operation just outside of Dallas, or in any part of the country where a club wishes to have such a program put on. For information, you may contact NAPD competition division, Rt. 2, Box 17BR, Lancaster, Texas 75146.

In the northeastern United States, you may contact Bob Turner, RACEWELD, 421 Marble Dr., Coraopolis, PA. 15108. Bob is a dentist by trade, and a race car fabricator by choice. He can also build you whatever trick metal work your heart desires.

The Body

The way our body fits in a car has a great deal to do with the way we drive, or are capable of driving. Some cars just cannot be driven by certain people. Our associate Phillip Harrelson simply cannot fit in most sports cars. At six feet six inches tall, and weighing three hundred pounds, he fills up the whole front seat of many sports cars, and cannot turn the wheel or reach the pedals due to a small driving compartment, versus Phillip. On the other side of the coin, Lisa Fletcher at slightly over five feet tall, and almost 100 pounds wringing wet, can fit neatly into even the smallest driving compartment.

When it comes to autocrossing, as is true in racing, the smaller a driver, the better chance for a win. Weight alone comprises a detriment in an autocross car. At six feet four inches tall, and two hundred fifty pounds, Dick Turner is approximately ten percent of the total weight of a competitive car. Assume a head to head competition with Lisa in identical cars. Dick has to overcome a one hundred fifty pound weight advantage held by Lisa. Assuming comparable driving ability, Lisa should win nearly every time out.

Once you are seated, move to a position where your arms and legs are slightly bent. Be sure you can reach the pedals, gearshift, and see out the windshield. If your seat back adjusts, position yourself so you can move freely and still be in a position to fasten your body tightly into the seat. We personally prefer to be fastened very tightly. A prime reason is to keep your body firm in the seat, and not have to support your torso with your hands on the steering wheel.

Body support from the steering wheel is a common trait among first time competitors. As a tip, if you have an inertia type seat belt, you can build yourself a quick release clamp to fit over your seat belt, thus holding the lower part of your body firmly in the seat.

As a comparison test, drive your car around a corner with the seat belt loosely fastened. Feel the side to side motion of your body. Now pull your belt as tight as you can. If a friend is near, have them pull on the belt from outside your car with the door open. Try the same corner and feel the difference. When we autocross, we take turns pulling belts tight for each other. Once we are fastened in, only hitting the release will allow even a slight movement.

The Head

Our head is usually thought of in a mental, rather than physical sense. For a moment, let's look at our head as physically capable, and in fact, carrying the necessary mechanism with which to make decisions and act in a closed circuit system of information gathering, analysis, decision making and guidance of our hands and feet. This mechanism is our brain. How do we gather information? The five senses are methods our brain uses to gather information it wishes to analyze. For example, we **see** a pylon in front of us. We **hear** our engine turning, and judge rpm's by the sound. We **feel** the car react under us. We also can **smell** a fuel leak on top of our engine (assuming such a leak exists). On rare occasions, we may **taste** a liquid to determine if it is really water! Granted, the last two senses are not used as much as the first three.

How do we use these senses? What does the input say, and how we do make an analysis, decision, and perform an action based on the decision? One important factor is to gather information from a known source, judged and proven by facts we have accurate knowledge of.

In solo competition, keeping our head erect will allow our eyes to perceive information correctly and transfer accurate information to the analysis "department" of our brain. Try looking at an object and judging its distance from your eyes. Now tilt your head to the side and try to reach a similar judgement while looking at another object.

Our brain is used to receiving information fed from an upright head position. When we tilt our head, as many of us do while autocrossing, we feed inaccurate information into our

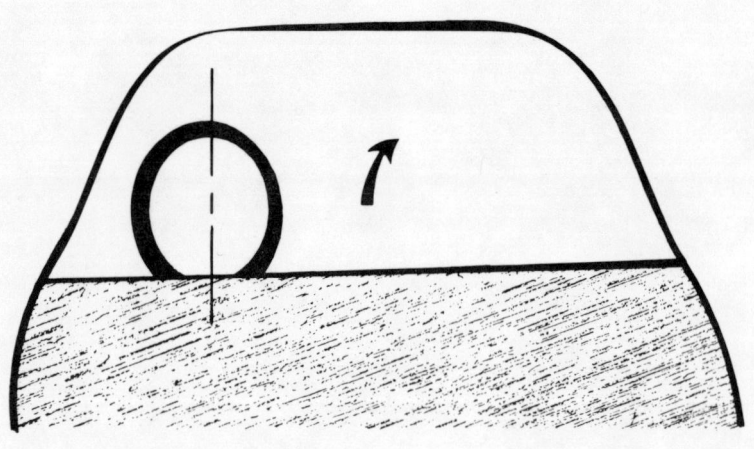

An upright head feeds information to our brain accurately. If we lean our head into a corner, the reference point changes, and our driving accuracy is reduced.

brain. If this input is wrong, then analysis and decisions will also be wrong. The result is a pylon being knocked over when you "just knew" you were far enough away to miss it.

Proper head positions play a vital role in autocross driving. If you find yourself leaning into a turn, sit back up and reexamine your position on the track. Ideally, each pylon will be nearly touched as we pass by, thus taking the shortest distance between gates. Only accurate vehicle placement can save time, and as with a telescopic rifle sight, a canted view decreases our accuracy.

The Hands

Second only to our brain in overall physical and mental priorities are our hands. We certainly agree that any part of our body is inferior to our brain; however, the way we control our hands is a terribly important part of autocrossing.

Hand placement on our steering wheel is critical. If we are driving in a straight line, our hands need to be at the nine o'clock and three o'clock positions. This position might just seem a little awkward to some people when first learning, but soon becomes second nature. If you have a car with a steering wheel as shown in our example, lock your thumbs over the crossbar while traveling in a straight line.

This position allows your arms to be in a strong position on your steering wheel, and will allow you to balance your upper body more correctly in your car. We strongly warn against bracing yourself with your steering wheel. However, the wheel can be an aid for fine tuning your body position relative to your car.

Your body should be far enough from your steering wheel that your arms are slightly bent, so you can turn your wheel 180 degrees without having to let go and then regrasp your wheel. At a position too short or too far from the wheel, your efficiency is reduced, and run times will suffer. Your gearshift lever should be within easy reach. We realize some cars have a shifting lever in a weird position. If this is the case in your car, be sure your steering is comfortable first, then work on your gearshift position. In solo competition, we know we will have to do a great deal of steering, as compared to a relatively small amount of shifting. Therefore, if we have to make a priority

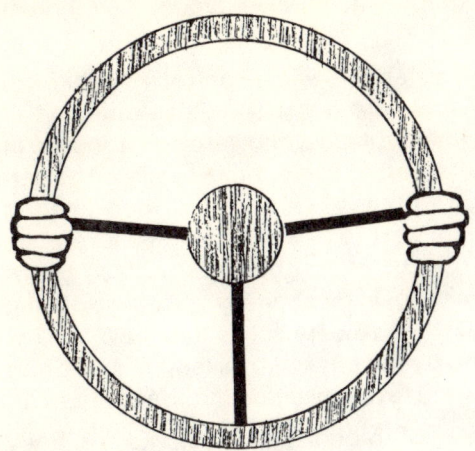

While traveling in a straight line, keep your hands at three o'clock and nine o'clock on the steering wheel. By doing so your arms are in a strong position and your upper body balanced.

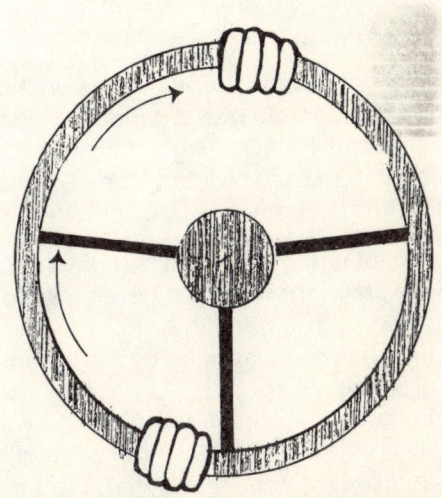

As you approach a corner, move your hands so that you will be at three o'clock and nine o'clock in the corner. By getting your hands set prior to corner entry, one less decision is required during the cornering maneuver.

judgement, we'll pick steering as number one and shifting as number two.

Since our hands on a steering wheel control a mechanical system, we are reasonably sure our wish is the command of many pounds of metal, glass, plastic, and assorted goodies. In a mechanical system, any part linked directly to any other part can cause movement. In driving, each part of our steering linkage works off another part until we reach track level. The relationship between our tires and the track surface is our weakest link. Our tires are not in mechanical harmony with the track surface, and can therefore only act as they have ability. That ability is controlled by the physical makeup of a tire and its connection with all other systems and functions of our car.

Newton's First Law of Motion tells us, "Every body continues in its state of rest, or of uniform motion in a straight line, unless it is compelled to change that state by forces impressed upon it." In simple terms, what Newton said was that a car being propelled in a straight line would rather continue on its path than change to another direction of its own volition. To change direction, a car needs an outside force. In a normal situation, our steering wheel, turned by our hands, causes a change in direction. The key to exactly how much of a turn we make is our tractive force at the front wheels. If our tires have sufficient bite on the road surface to carry out commands, our car will turn as requested. If our tires do not have enough force, the front wheels slip, causing our car to understeer.

Let's consider our hands on a steering wheel as a pebble dropped into a glassy smooth pond. Circles form as a pebble strikes the water. Each circle moves outward becoming larger as it travels. The circle finally smoothes out again, starting from the spot where our pebble hit.

Steering input can be compared to our pebble. As we turn our steering wheel, we have an action equivalent to our pebble hitting the water. An entry into a serene motion, the straight line, has been induced by a mechanical means. As we turn our steering wheel, let's say to our left, many different factors become involved. First, our front wheels move left, since they as a connected part of our system. As our tires move, speed and overall adhesion come into play. If our tires can absorb and transmit enough energy to the road surface, and not pass a point of ultimate adhesion, we begin to move left. At this same time, our right side suspension begins to compress, and our left side suspension parts begin to stretch. Compression continues until a point is reached where the accelerative motion to our right is compensated for by our right side springs, torsion bars, or whatever means of suspension we have. If we have turned in a smooth arc, our suspension reaches a maximum loading point of no return, stops, and travels in the other direction. What we have done, is produced a series of ripples traveling from one end of our suspension to the other.

If we move our hands at the slowest possible rate, we put only as much pressure on our suspension parts as is necessary to produce an output equal to our input.

We could carry this discussion to many other parts of our suspension system, and even to torquing of our chassis under extreme loading. To understand our point, let's make a suspension system as simple as is practically possible. The total suspension consists of two springs at each corner of our car. Spring number one is our normally thought of spring. For sake of discussion, let's call any form of recoiling mechanism a spring. This main spring is supposed to support weight, and compress in a corner, or under braking or accelerating conditions. We will all readily accept this form of energy transfer device.

What many people do not realize is that we have another spring at each corner of our car. This spring conceals its identity however, and is known to us as a tire. Yes, our tires are springs. Depending on which type of tire we have, we may have a spring with considerable travel, or one with relatively little travel. Nonetheless, tires are springs.

When figuring a spring rate for a vehicle, tires must be taken into account, or your rating will be in error. A tire change can also greatly affect a spring rating. Some people change tires, never thinking about the overall effects on their springing system. To do so causes losses at the track.

Let's examine a spring to show overloading and reactions caused from such an overload. Our coil spring in this example will start at a height of fifteen inches, standing on a workbench. We will call this height our design height.

Next, we will install our spring in a car. The height now is decreased by four inches, for sake of discussion. We will refer to this height as our installed height.

Now, we will drive a car around a medium hard corner, and induce a gravity load of .4g. In this condition, our spring has

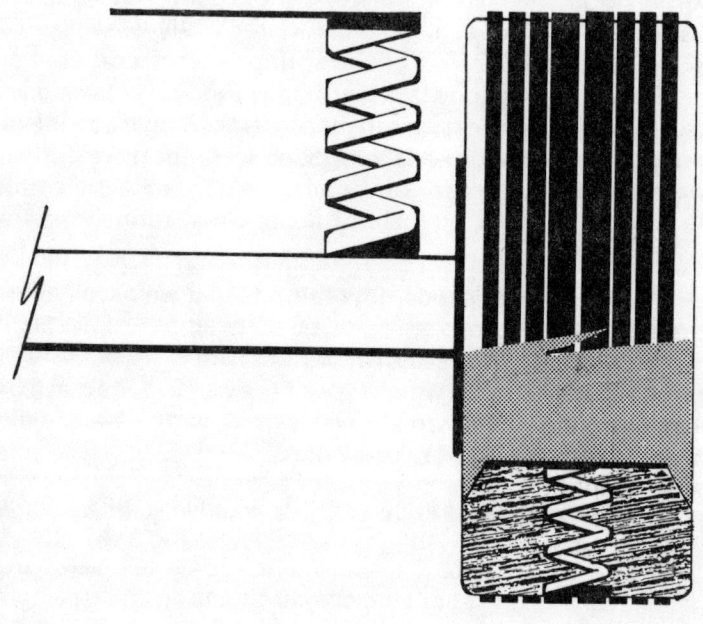

Many people do not realize tires are a form of spring. Your tires are the first point of movement with regard to a track surface, and as such are a vital part of your suspension.

compressed to a height of eight inches. We will call this height .4g compression.

We will now travel the same corner, only we will jerk our steering wheel, compressing our spring to a height of six inches, and completely closing all coils. This is referred to as total compression height.

As we jerked our car into the corner, not only did our spring compress to its maximum point we also have compressed our tire in the process.

We can compare our fifteen inch design height and six inch total compression height, and call all the distance between these two points "travel". Our spring has a total travel potential of nine inches. If we drive properly, we will cause a travel height decrease of six inches. We derive our figure from an eleven inch installed height and a .4g compression height of eight inches.

If we steer smoothly, our car starts at an eleven inch installed height, moves into a corner at exactly .4g, and compresses to a height of eight inches. As we steer out of our corner, we now move back to an eleven inch height.

Conversely, if we jerk our car into the same corner, our compression travels to its limit, then leans on our tire. The result will be a direction change, and if our corner is short enough, such as negotiating a tight slalom, we will be turning in the other direction as our reaction takes place. Since we overload our spring while turning left, as we turn right we have not only the action of a new direction of travel, but an acceleration caused by overloading our spring to begin with. As our spring rebounds, we can actually cause it to travel past the fifteen inch design height, and stretch. If we consider a stretch of three inches past our design height, we have induced an actual suspension travel of twelve inches. Obviously, three inches of travel versus twelve inches can make a tremendous difference in a corner.

How we move our hands is the controlling factor. Rapid, jerky movement will cause far too much suspension travel. Slow, fluid movement will cause only needed suspension travel.

We have **never** had a student move his or her hands as slowly as need be when a class started. Only constant mental awareness coupled with physical practice can result in slow hands.

Try to be conscious of your hand motion every time you drive your car. Think about moving as slowly on your steering

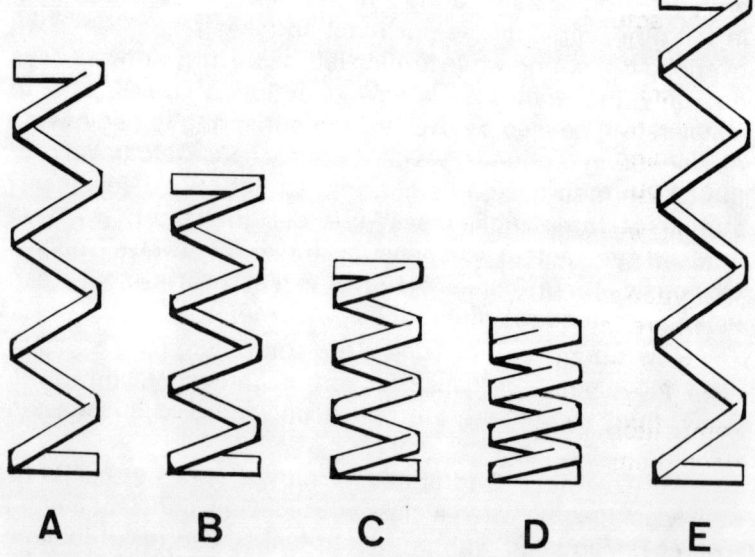

Smoothness eliminates excess spring travel. (A) shows the design height, (B) installed height, (C) .4g turn height, (D) total compression height, and (E) stretched height.

wheel as possible, and still take the intended direction of travel. As you corner, move your hands so slowly that you think you will not make the corner. Try driving around a corner at an extremely low speed. Be conscious of your rate of steering input. Now, drive around the same corner at twice the original speed, but move your hands at exactly the same rate of speed as you did originally. Keep increasing your speed until you reach a maximum adhesion limit.

Once you have learned the secret of slow hands, you'll kick yourself for not figuring it out on your own. In years past, when we raced very seriously, we would watch other drivers fight a car lap after lap. In those days, the name of the game was winning, and as a result, we didn't run over and tell them how to correct their problem. Why more people don't know this secret, we cannot explain. We can tell you this: it wins trophies! Think about squeezing your car through a corner. Only apply as much steering as is required. If your car starts to slip, correct it only slightly faster than you steered into the corner before slipping. By making slow, deliberate movements, you always know where you began to lose tractive forces, and can go back easily to a corrective point.

As you approach a corner, think about the position your hands will be in during the cornering move. While you are still traveling in a straight line, position your hands on the wheel so as you actually begin to corner, your hands will move to the three o'clock and nine o'clock position at the apex.

Since we need most careful control of our car in the corner, not on the straight just prior to corner entry, positioning your hands ahead of time gives positive control when you need it most.

Likewise, as you leave the corner, move your hands one at a time to bring your car slowly and smoothly out onto the next straightaway. This method of steering can be practiced anywhere, not just while in competition.

Slow down and you'll go faster. Sounds like a dumb statement, but if you will learn the secret, then apply it, other competitors will wonder why your car does things theirs won't. Keep them guessing, stay confident, and win.

The Feet

Second only to hand movement is what we do with our feet. Feet primarily affect the pitch motion of our vehicle by using either our accelerator, or our brakes.

If we jump on the accelerator, various results occur, depending on the horsepower of a car. With a low horsepower vehicle, the lack of power will cause little tractive effect. However, with a car such as J.B.'s modified Pantera, if you jump on the accelerator, 550 horses will give you an instant lesson in what not to do. If done properly though, the Pan will react like a pussy cat, albeit a kind you respect highly.

Another phenomenon taking place when you apply the accelerator too fast is known as cold wall quenching. As we rapidly depress our accelerator, an accelerator pump forces a shot of liquid fuel into the combustion chamber. As this happens, fuel condenses on the sides of the cylinder. This is one cause for the momentary delay in building rpm's.

If we examine the properties of liquid gasoline, we find it does not burn. Only gasoline in combination with air will burn. When we refer to air, the oxygen content of air is what gives the needed addition to create an explosion. If such is the case, it can be readily understood that a shot of raw fuel will only slow down your engine until there has been a sufficient amount of oxygen added to burn off excess liquid. This whole process is measured in hundredths of a second, but isn't that what we are looking for?

Have you ever seen a car that can go from zero to twenty miles-per-hour in two-tenths of a second? Obviously the answer is no. If this is true, then why do we try to push our

26

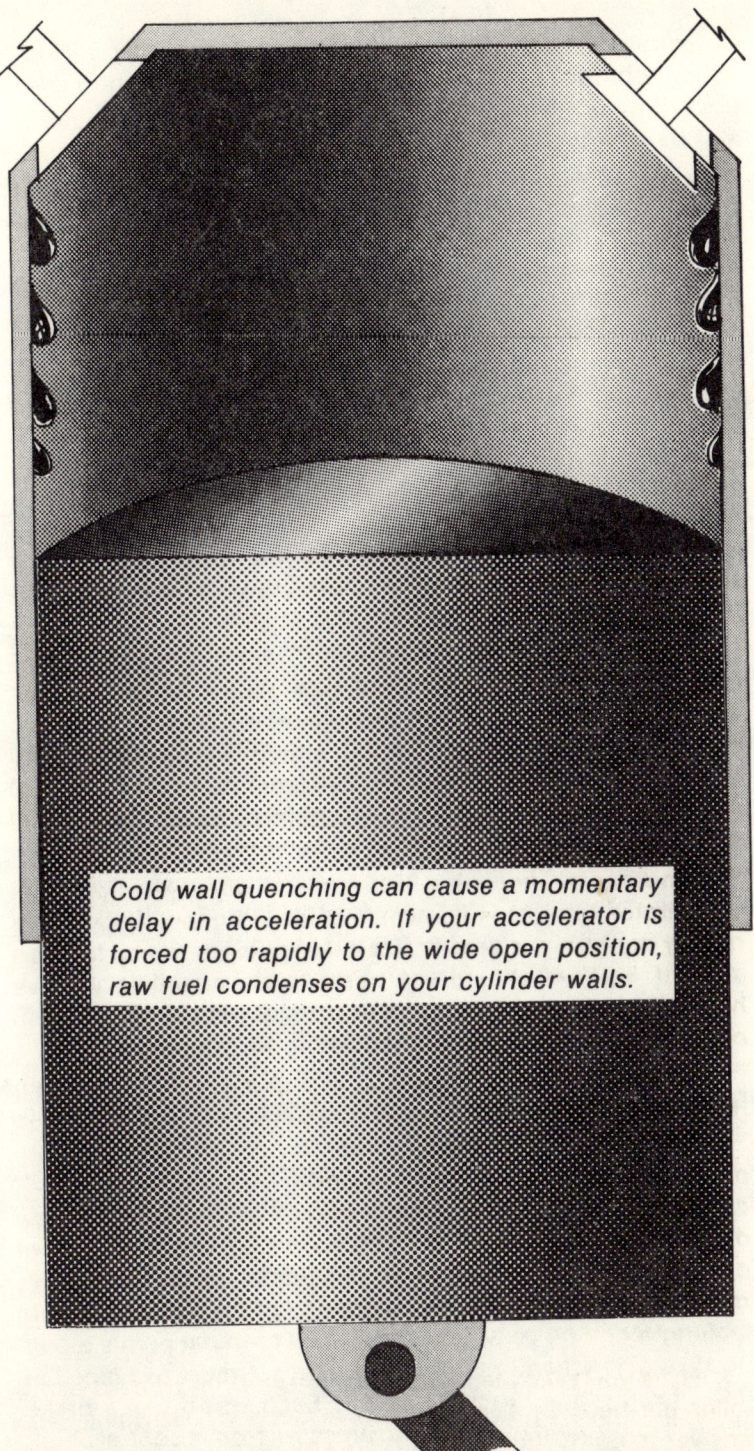

Cold wall quenching can cause a momentary delay in acceleration. If your accelerator is forced too rapidly to the wide open position, raw fuel condenses on your cylinder walls.

accelerator past the front bumper as we leave the starting line? In two-tenths of a second, you can push your accelerator to the floor. Why not slow the action down to seven or eight tenths and be smooth?

In a super strong car, we are creating another problem if we push our accelerator to the floor. At some point between idle and on the floor, our rear wheels are going to break traction. If we have jumped on the accelerator, our only alternative is to jump off when this occurs. Our car then comes back in shape, and we jump again. If at this point we are moving fast enough, we may get away with it a second time. We know of one car-driver combination that has done this since the first time we saw him run. He has an extremely strong car, and jumps, lurches and screams from pylon to pylon. To date, no one in his class has been able to make up for his tremendous horsepower and he feels he is doing a good job. We've never been able to figure out why he doesn't get the picture, though, when smaller, weaker cars take top-time-of day at practically every event.

Once you are off the line and rolling, what next? By squeezing your accelerator, the front end of your car does not rise as rapidly, and the rear end maintains traction. What is actually happening if we could watch our car move in milliseconds would shock even the pros. As a car pulls, the front end rises. If the rear tires begin to spin, there is an instantaneous loss of traction, and the front end falls slightly. As your tires regain bite the nose rises. This process looks like a bucking bronco, as compared to providing your tires with all the power they can handle, but not overdoing it.

This same action in reverse takes place when you shut down for a corner. The nose falls rapidly when you come off your accelerator quickly. As this happens, your car bounces on the front suspension, and the rear end gets light. By taking five or six tenths to remove power, the nose settles rather than dives.

At this point you may be saying, "Fine, but what about brakes?" Brakes are the second part of your "foot system." Let's examine how and why brakes do what they do.

Modern brakes operate on the theory of Paschal's law, which briefly states: "In an enclosed fluid system, pressure applied to one point will be equal at all terminal points along the system." Accepting this law as true, we must examine the basic design of a braking system. Each wheel has a brake which is controlled by hydraulic pressure from a central point, or the master cylinder.

Under heavy acceleration our car rises in the front, and falls in the rear. Smooth application of power makes the move less violent, especially in a high powered machine. With front wheel drive, the same action takes place, but the rise in front is usually less, as is the corresponding fall in the rear.

Under heavy braking our car falls in the front, and rises in the rear. Smooth application of our brakes keeps the front end from bouncing on the suspension, thus maintaining maximum traction on all four tires.

The master cylinder in many cars is divided into two sections, one serving your front wheels, and another section serving your rear wheels. You will notice by visual examination that the front section is somewhat larger than the rear. This is due to the fact that approximately sixty percent of all braking force in your car comes from the front brakes. If this is true, then our braking system must be telling us something about weight shift.

As a car is slowed by braking, the rolling weight shifts forward. When this happens, your front suspension is compressed. If the front end is compressing, the rear end must be stretching, or rising. This means your front tires will have far more traction than the rear tires. Heavy braking will result in locked rear tires. This causes the car to get very uneasy, and if the condition is not corrected immediately, we are in a skid.

Let's consider left foot braking for a moment, then expand into a quick way through most autocross corners. Most people in Solo II and autocross competition try to use some form of heel and toe, or they may lift their right foot off the accelerator, and put it on the brake.

In most autocrosses, shifting is done relatively few times during a run. In our opinion, most drivers shift far too many times to begin with. If we examine a run, most cars start out in first gear. When you pull a second gear shift, in effect, you will have to shift twice. Since most events have faster sections, then slower sections, you will probably have to return to low gear. The key to victory is knowing the net difference between shifting, and remaining in an existing gear at red line for a short stretch. It feels like forever if you have to travel for a second at red line, rather than keep busy shifting to the next higher gear, then back again. What must be weighed carefully is the time required to make two shifts, amount of time pulling in the higher gear, amount of brake lag before you can shift back down without overreving, and the balance of your car during the process. By balance we are referring to our car placed squarely on all four tires, rather than rocking back and forth from one position to another.

Most of us feel we are accomplishing great things when we are straining, hanging on the edge of oblivion, tires screaming, car reacting wildly, and sweating like a horse. Watch Mario Andretti drive. He looks like his car is on a rail, and moving him, rather than the opposite. Mario rarely makes a mistake, and when he does, he is criticized for running far too fast. The man isn't running too fast, he's just superior to any car under him,

and is squeezing out every last ounce of performance. When he finally crosses the upper adhesion limit, it looks like a cannon went off. A true autocross or Solo II champion looks slow and methodical until you see his or her time. At NAPD, we have a saying: "You can run for go, or play for show, but not both." Make up your mind which it will be, because you can't do both and win. If you want to be a winner, the only spectacular part of watching you will be the end result. To the uninitiated, you'll be a drag to watch. To good competitors, you'll be the hero or heroine of the crowd.

Shifting

It might seem elementary to talk about shifting in a book about advanced autocrossing. However, the method used for shifting and overall efficiency of each shift has a great deal to do with our time on a run, and thus fits into a picture of the total autocross driver.

As you leave the starting gate, let your clutch out with a smooth steady motion. Don't 'dump' the clutch as is sometimes done in drag racing. We don't mean to ease the clutch pedal out, unless you have an immediate sharp turn, and are driving a high powered car. In an autocross, it pays to rev your engine a little higher than normal to insure that your car does not die coming off the line. As you reach each shift point of your tach, learn to bring the rpm's down to the pulling point of the next gear. By so doing, you will be less apt to cause an imbalance in the car as you change gears.

Downshifting requires a slightly different technique. We prefer to use the double clutch method. By double clutching, we mean a maneuver that goes as follows. Push in on the clutch pedal, and pull the shift lever into neutral. Release the clutch, and build your rpm's to match the needed level for the next lower gear. If you are going to jump two gears, know what rpm you need to reach before attempting to shift. When you have matched the rpm required, push the clutch back in, shift into the gear, and release the clutch.

By utilizing this method, you will create far less driveline strain and you'll be less apt to miss a shift.

As you move from one gear to another, whether up, or down, don't have a fight with the shift lever. Move in a firm, but

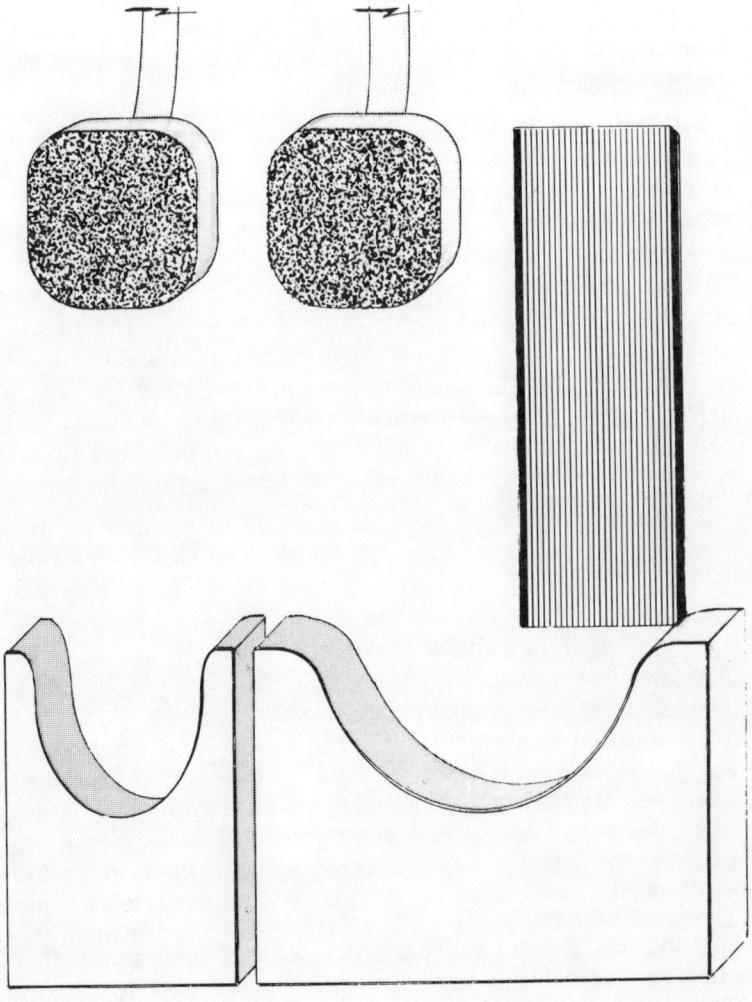

By making two blocks, one for each foot, you can keep your feet firmly planted during a run. Notice that our right block is slightly larger to allow free movement from the brake to accelerator.

gentle manner. If you cram the car in gear, driveline torque will imbalance your car, and there is always the chance that you can bend a synchronizer and end up in a mess.

As you shift, you may wish to employ a heel-and-toe style, especially when you need heavy braking and a shift at the same time. The term is somewhat of a misnomer, since in many cars you are not actually using your heel and toe. If your pedals are close enough together, the left side of your right foot will operate the brake, while the right side of your foot is on the accelerator.

If your car should be set up in a manner that requires actual use of the heel and toe, use this basic thought as a guideline — use your toes for the strongest part of the system. What we mean by this is to put your heel on the accelerator, and your toes on the brake if you have a low horsepower car. With a high powered machine, put your heel on the brake, and your toes on the accelerator. Our toes have more feeling and more flexibility than our heel. With a low powered car, we can run a little deeper into a corner, then be sensitive on our brakes to avoid going into a skid; whereas with a high powered car, we can pull off a corner with great speed, and therefore do not want the car getting squirrely under acceleration.

Another little ploy you may use is to build two small platforms for your feet. One can be placed to keep your right foot in a position for proper control of the brake and accelerator. This can be a block of wood cut to the shape of the back of your driving shoes. Make the block just high enough to give your heel the support it needs to fit exactly in the same place each time you make your move. We should point out that it is important to always race in the same pair of shoes, or, if you have more than one pair, be sure they are identical. By doing this, you will learn the feel of the road through your feet, and can better judge the point of incipient skid and the maximum power point under heavy acceleration.

A method we have used that works well as a time saver is to find the exact point at which your clutch disengages, then push your pedal one half inch further and measure from the floorboard to the back side of your clutch pedal. Build a block of wood to fit in this space. On top of the block place a one half inch thick piece of sponge rubber. This will allow room for the clutch to disengage, but will not waste motion and time between gears. Some cars have a tremendous amount of slack between the disengagement point and floorboard. Once the clutch has disengaged, everything else is wasted motion.

Push your clutch pedal to the point of disengagement. Add another ½ inch for safety, and measure this distance from the floorboard. Build a block to fit under the pedal at the height you measured. Glue a ½ inch piece of sponge rubber on top of the block and mount it under your clutch pedal. This will eliminate excess travel each time you shift.

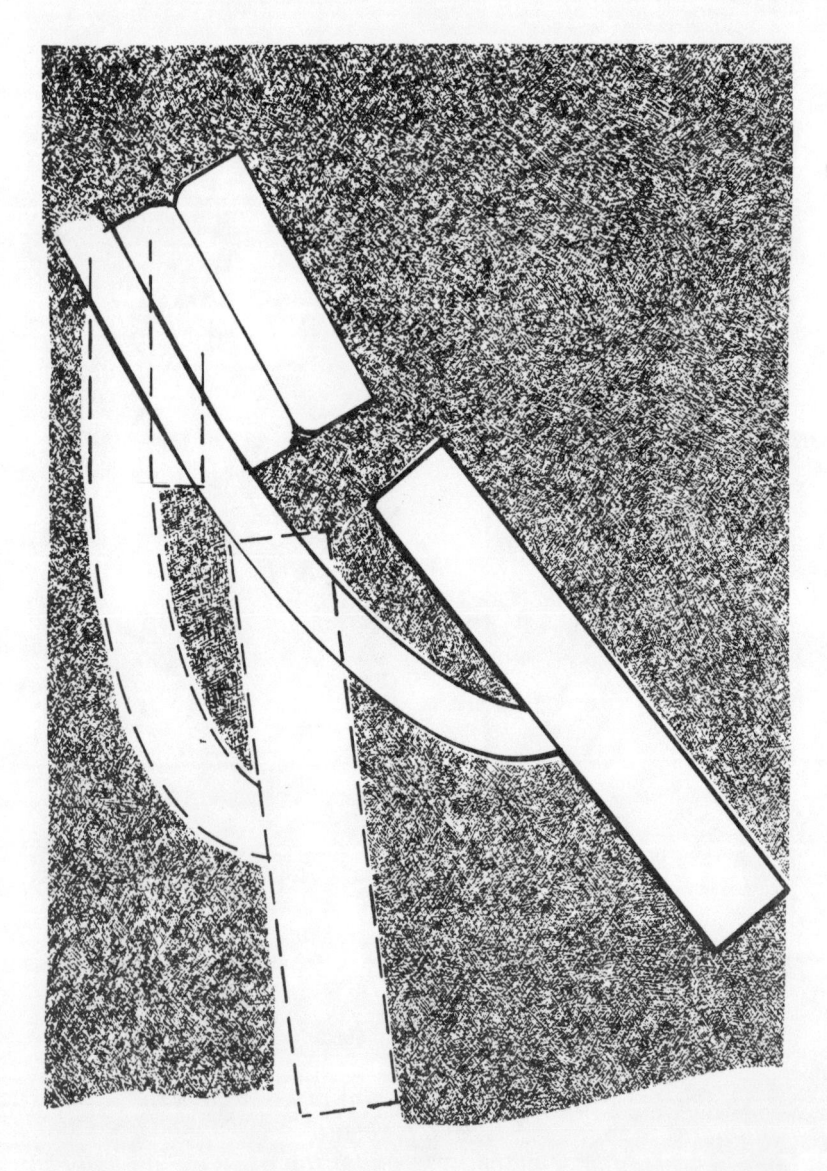

A block can be fashioned to eliminate excess brake travel at the brakes off position. Just be sure you are not applying brake pressure with the block!

This is also true to some extent in the adjustment of your brake pedal. You may want to build a small block to fit on top of the pedal support, holding it just above the contact point of your pads.

These methods of tuning your car can add to your overall efficiency, and efficiency measures out in time saved.

Accelerating and Braking Forces

If asked about acceleration and braking, most of us would be quick to think about acceleration forces created by our engine, and stopping power of our brakes. These are, of course, the main forces acting on our car; but in a solo event, lay of the land can have a great effect.

When you walk a course prior to running an event, forget about what you did last night, or how dumb these walkthroughs seem to you. Examine every inch of the surface for possible gains of acceleration, or hinderances in braking. For example, an asphalt patch on a concrete surface will give you less stopping power than a concrete patch on an asphalt surface. With a concrete patch however, be careful of exposed edges in a patched area. Since concrete is a rigid surface material, asphalt may wear away from the edge, and a tire cut can ruin your run.

The other side of the coin is a hinderance in acceleration, or chance for some stronger braking. On an uneven surface, you might gain a couple thousandths on a downhill section, but be careful since it will take more stopping power from the same speed than it will on a level surface. Likewise, an uphill run will increase your braking ability while slowing down your top speed for the distance between pylons.

If you run autocross near an ocean, watch for slickness produced by salt air. Wind also can be a factor. The list can go on almost indefinitely, but bear in mind, an aware racer is usually a fast racer.

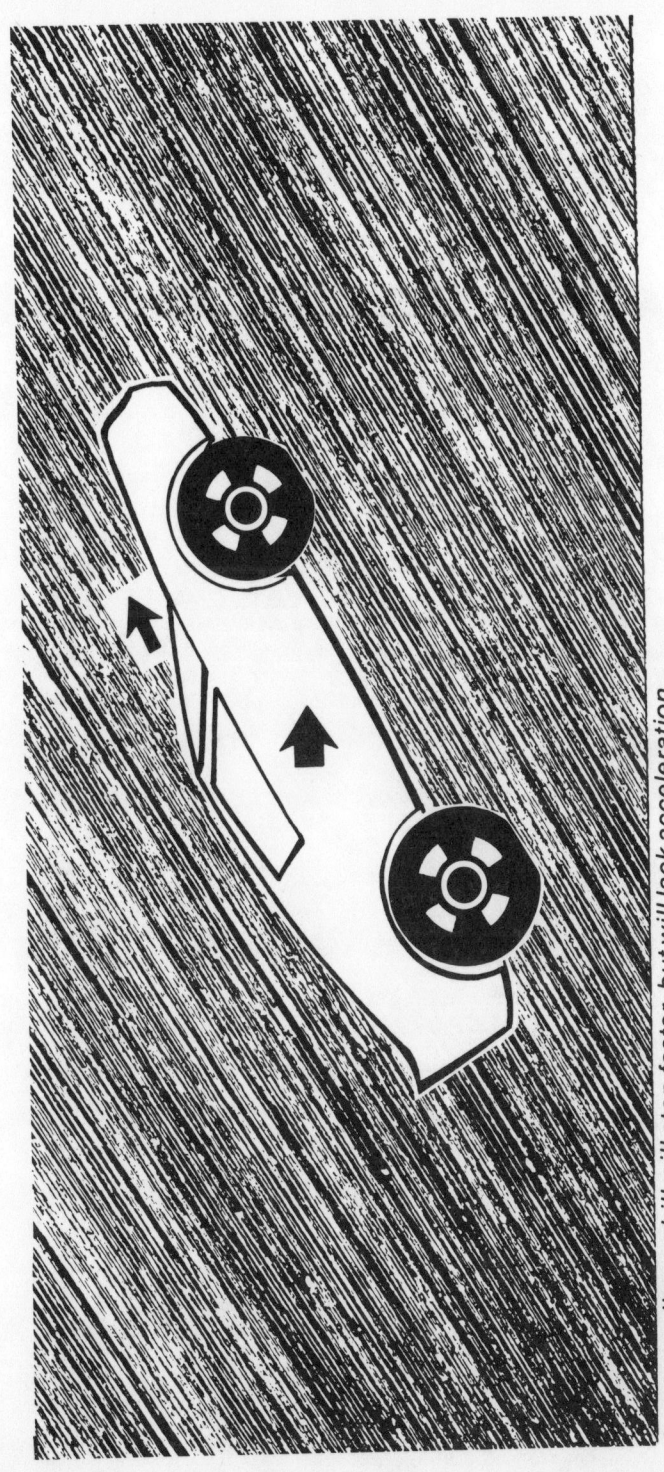

A car traveling uphill will stop faster, but will lack acceleration. Not only does the angle of the hill work against your car, the force of gravity remains constant. As a result we are trying to drive into the hill as well as up.

A car traveling downhill lacks braking power, but will accelerate very rapidly. Do not make the mistake of running too deep into a downhill turn. Heavy application of brakes while traveling in a downhill position will result in a severe understeer condition.

Basic Suspension Functions

A suspension system in an autocross car is very much of a compromise. One end of the scale gives us roadholding characteristics, while the other end gives us ride quality.

The main thought to bear in mind is that all four wheels should remain in ground contact at all times. Under cornering stress, a major part of your car's weight is transferred to the outside wheels. It is far more important to keep your outside wheels on the ground than it is to keep your inside front wheel stable.

The toughest problem to overcome with a super stiff suspension is actual tire patch contact with the road surface at any given time. If a suspension is too stiff, your tires only touch high spots on the track, thus leaving a lot to be desired in the adhesion department. The best compromise is a semi soft suspension with highly efficient dampening devices. Good shock absorbers are a must for your Solo II car.

The major factors to consider are overall weight, distribution of weight, wheelbase and track, ratio of sprung to unsprung mass, suspension design, height of the center of gravity, roll center heights at both front and rear of the car, steering geometry—and the elusive factor, tires.

Tires affect roadholding, and, with wheels and hubs, comprise the major unsprung weight in your car. If possible, we want unsprung weight as low as possible to reduce bump steer, or the effect of momentum with respect to an undulating road surface.

The average autocross car has a suspension you cannot change drastically according to the rules, but for those of you

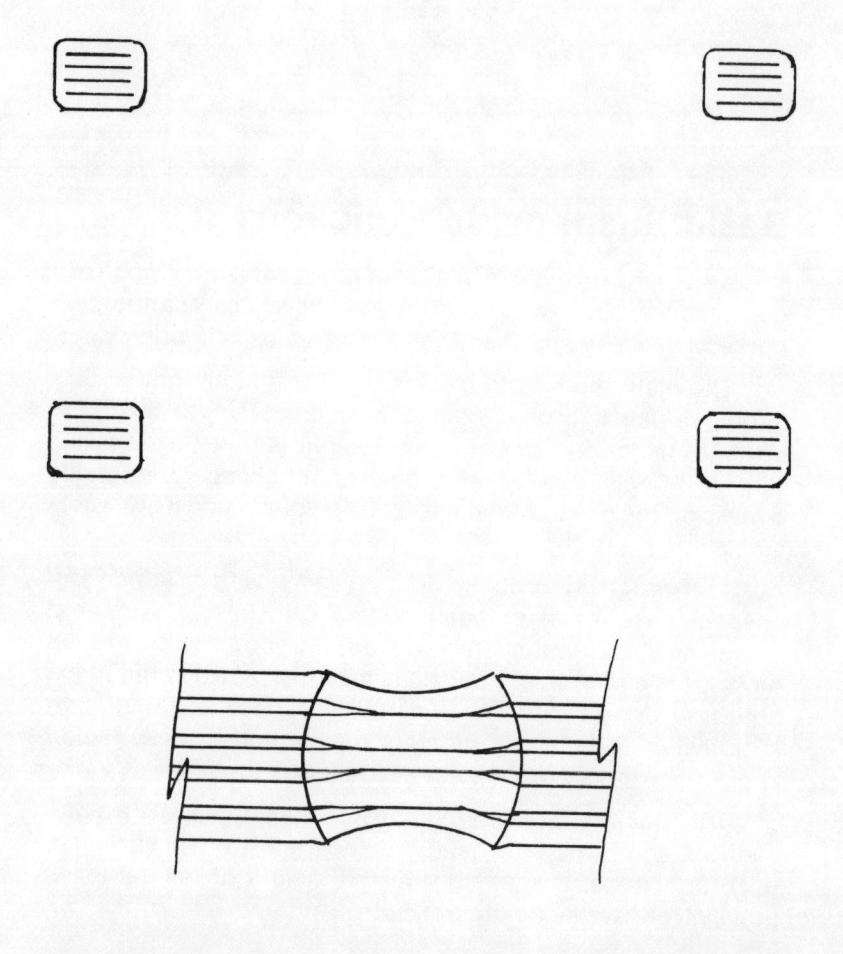

The top illustration shows our tire patch, or control points on the track. It is easy for us to forget that our whole car rides on these four small patches of rubber.

Our bottom illustration shows the effect of tire squirm. With a radial tire, squirm is reduced. Our illustration compares best with a bias ply tire. As you can see, traction is greatly decreased due to the closed tread area.

who run exotic 'home-builts,' carefully consider using inboard brakes if possible to reduce the unsprung mass. Brakes when mounted inboard tend to overheat sooner than outboard, but this problem is not critical on an autocross car since run times are short with ample cooling between runs.

The center of gravity has an effect on a suspension package and roadholding ability of your car. If we were to look at a solid cube of steel, it would be easy to understand center of gravity as the exact center of the block. With a car, position from front to back and height above the ground are major measuring factors. It is very easy for the center of gravity of an autocross car to be off center, and in front of or behind the center of a car as measured from either end. If we could design the perfect suspension, center of gravity would be at ground level, exactly centered in the car. As soon as we move from this position, we are compromising.

Newton's first law of motion shows us how a car turns. The center of gravity would like to travel in a straight line, but a slip angle induced through steering makes our car accelerate toward the center of a circle or arc created by steering action. If our car were being held in place by a cable connected to the center of gravity, there would be no side loading factor on the tires. If the cable were cut, our car immediately would travel in a straight line to the tangent of the circle.

If we now drive our car around a circle, a side thrust is created by the slip angle of our front tires applied through the center of gravity. Since our front wheels are doing the turning, overall slip angle is greater at the front of our car. This means a neutral handling car when driven too hard will tend to understeer.

Weight transfer is another factor to contend with when autocrossing. Actual transfer is caused by centrifugal force acting through the center of gravity, being resisted by adhesion characteristics of our tires. The result is a weight shift to the outside tires, thus creating a lifting force on our inside wheels and an increase in weight on the outside wheels.

Wheel rigidity is another factor often overlooked by the average autocrosser. Cast magnesium wheels have the greatest rigidity, and based on this criteria would rate as most desireable. Magnesium wheels are also considerably lighter than steel or spoked wheels, and thus help reduce the unsprung weight of our car.

Springs have a great effect on roadholding. The amount of

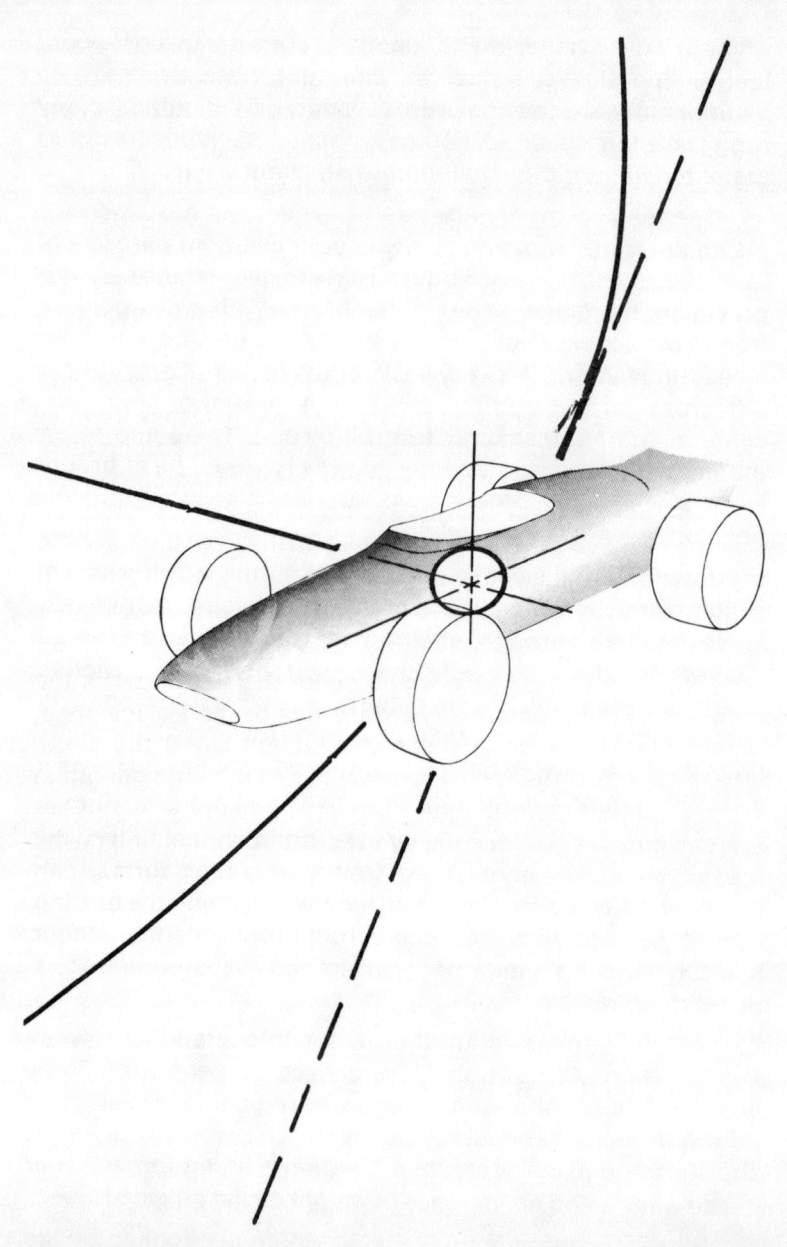

The inward force in our illustration is centripetal force. Our car is under control of centripetal force created by the road acting in a manner to hold our car. The outward force is centrifugal force, created by our car. If the cable holding our car in the illustration were to break, the car would go off at a tangent to the circle, or in a straight line - just like our old friend Mr. Newton said it would!

stiffness must be tempered with ability of the spring rate to keep all four tires on the ground. The correct rate will allow any given wheel to rise without effecting the car. Too strong — car bounces; too weak — suspension bounces. Neither characteristic will aid in cornering ability of a car.

Roll bars—more correctly called anti-roll bars—have a specific purpose but are often misunderstood and abused in application. The purpose of a roll bar is to reduce roll motion in the car and reduce changes in camber angles associated with excessive body roll.

A strong front roll bar reduces the rear end roll center due to a decreased roll angle at the front. A roll bar does transfer weight to the outside front wheel, however, and can create a condition of understeer. If a front bar cannot take care of the vehicle, then a rear bar may be added. It should be remembered that when adding a rear bar, the front bar needs to be stronger. Rigidity of the bar increases as the fourth power of its diameter. By balancing front and rear bars, handling is increased.

If such is the case, it would seem that a roll bar is the answer to all our problems. There are drawbacks. For instance, stiffer roll bars cause less sensitive action along the entire suspension. Another rare but possible situation is a bar going into resonance, since it is an undampened spring. A stiff bar also can adversely affect one wheel due to a connection on the opposite side of your car. Irregularities on a road surface can cause a loss of control from only one wheel striking a bump if the bar is strong enough to negate the balance of our suspension. Roll bars serve to assist rather than dominate a proper suspension.

Tires

Of all 'pieces' we can play with on an autocross car, tires have to rank number one as the least understood and most discussed part of racing.

There are three basic types of tires in use today: bias ply, bias ply belted, and radial ply. All three designs have certain parts in common. All types consist of a bead, cord body, and tread and side wall. The beads are two hoops, made of strong steel wire and tied to the cord body. They provide a seal to keep air in the tire. In the past, an inner tube did part of the job now accomplished by the bead. Older tires still had a bead, but it lacked air holding characteristics.

A cord body consists of numerous layers of cord bonded together to form one unit. We normally refer to cords as plies. Thus, a four ply tire has four layers of cord. Cords are made from rayon, nylon, polyester, aramid fiber, or steel. They are the supporting structure of a tire. The tread and sidewall are formed over cords in the process of building a tire. Rubber, synthetically produced, is laid over the cord body, then placed in a mold. The rubber is heated until it is molten where cooking takes place. The mold forms the molten rubber into a tread pattern. Thus many various sizes and styles can be found at any tire factory. Two or three designs from most manufacturers will work well in autocross.

Bias ply tires are on the way out, and are found mostly in cheaper lines. Construction consists of two to four layers of cord body layed up in a lattice work. Each layer is offset approximately 35 degrees from the other. A rubber interior lining covers a fabric casing to give tires air holding ability.

A bias ply belted tire starts out the same way, but between the top layer of bias cord and tread, two more belts of cord are layered under the tread area. They do not extend to the beads on either side. Their prime function is to help stabilize the tread and reduce internal stress on a tire. In addition, the tread surface has more wearing capability, and gives a more stable ride.

Radial ply tires are the most modern structure, and will most likely be the only type of quality tire offered within a few years. Radial ply tires have walls reinforced from bead to bead with cords strung radially, or across the tread. Standard radial design has two plies of cord. One problem associated with early radials was their harsh ride quality. This prompted use of only two plies, rather than four as had been the standard for years in bias ply tires. A belt laid under the tread area on a radial tire is comprised of a thicker, stronger cord, that resists stretching and reduces tire squirm. Squirm is nothing more than inability of a tread to remain properly shaped under stress, or compression. On a bias ply tire, the outer edges of the tread tend to squeeze toward the center tread pattern upon contact with a road surface. This reduces running area, or patch of the tire, and thus is an undersirable design for solo competition.

By comparison, belted radial tires resist squirming, and give a greater patch area on which to maneuver.

As a tire rolls, then turns at a request of the steering mechanism, the angle of a tire as compared to the direction of original travel is known as slip angle. Newtons First Law of Motion tries to keep a tire going in the original direction of travel, but mechanical steering turns a tire on the road surface. Greater steering input produces an increased slip angle of the tire. A tire traveling in a straight line has a slip angle of zero, while a tire in a tight turn around a pylon may have a slip angle of 20 degrees. At some point around 20 degrees, a tire is at maximum cornering ability. The exact maximum depends on tires, design, and road surface.

At this point we need to introduce another key factor. Slip angle produces a braking effect on the vehicle. By using a smooth trailing brake, combined with braking effect of the slip angle, we can run deeper into a turn, retain maximum speed longer, and be set up to hold a certain amount of force. A novice who corners and brakes hard at the same time is probably going to spin. Once a tire passes the maximum adhesion limit, its roadholding ability decreases drastically,

SLIP ANGLE

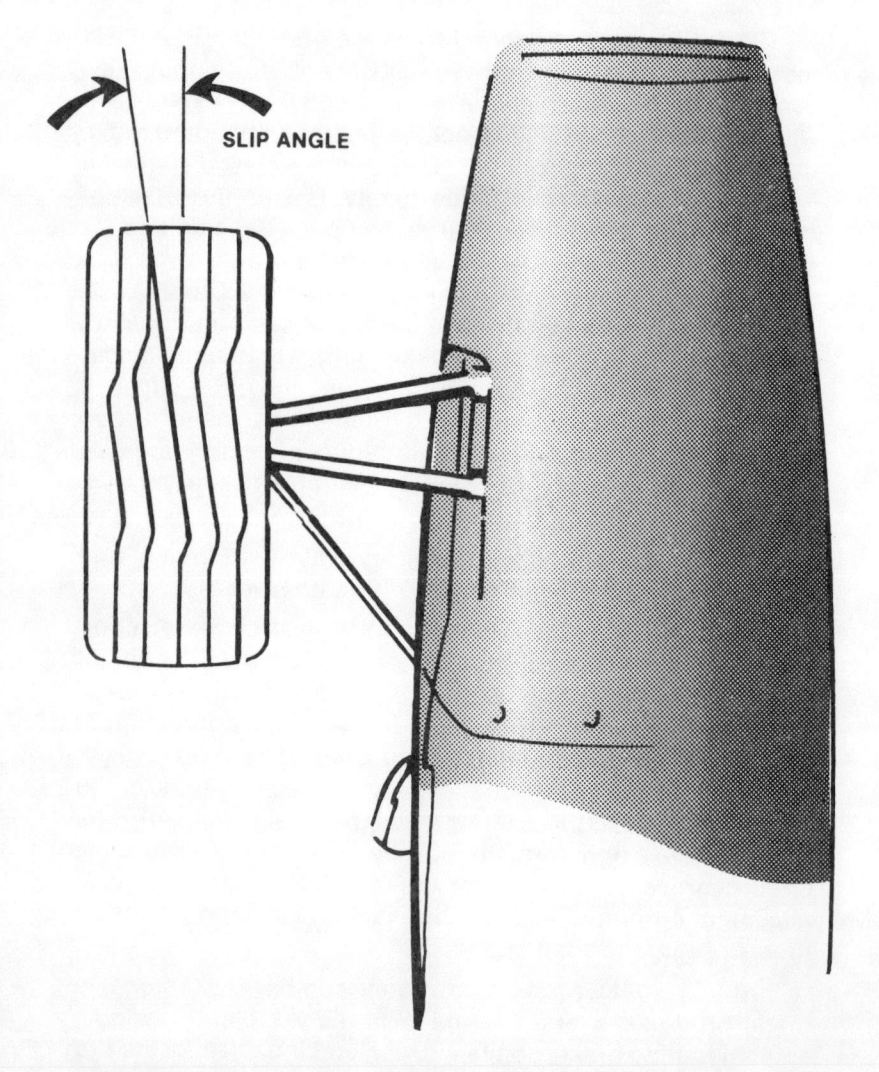

When rolling under the influence of a lateral load, the elasticity of a tire creates an angle between the actual direction of travel and the lag, or slip rate of the tread. As the tire rolls, a new patch of rubber is introduced to the track surface. With respect to the road surface, the patch is in a static position.

and very rapidly. If your tires are locked up, cornering force is reduced to zero and your car will travel in a straight line. By utilizing strong braking in a straight line, then a slip angle of close to 20 degrees with no brake pressure, while turning, your car still has approximately one third maximum possible braking effort and will corner without skidding.

Racing tires have improved tremendously in the past few years. In fact, tires are responsible for more track records than any other single element on a car. One problem that has developed for drivers is less feel at the point of incipient skid. The upper limit of lateral adhesion is reached with little or no warning, and once traction is broken, it is very tough to regain. If you run in a race/prepared class, learn the limits of your tires, and try to stay within the limits of maximum adhesion.

Conditioned Reflex Autocrossing and the Closed Loop System

The dictionary describes a conditioned reflex as "a reflex in which the response is occasioned by a secondary stimulus repeatedly associated with the primary stimulus." We all have heard of Dr. Pavlov and his experiments with dogs. How can we draw from his research and apply it to our sport?

If we examine 'a reflex in which the response' as a phrase, the response might be adrenalin flowing through our system. 'Occasioned by a secondary stimulus' can be completion of a perfect run. In other words, the run is our secondary stimulus. 'Repeatedly associated with the primary stimulus' can be our time, with reference to times of our competition. In other words, good time, produced because we did everything right, makes our adrenalin flow.

A closed loop system, for our purposes is a mental and physical situation in which the driver senses a need for a physical movement and makes that movement, which then causes our car to move. The driver then analyzes each move. If it is correct, he mentally moves on to something else. If a move is not correct, he then takes whatever physical action he feels is necessary to get to the correct position.

If we take the physical action of moving from a mode of acceleration to a mode of braking and constantly practice, we will become very good at each move. In fact, at some point in time the move will become automatic. At this point, the move has been programmed into our subconscious mind, and becomes a conditioned reflex. Without having consciously to determine what the car is doing, we can make a correction and go on about our run.

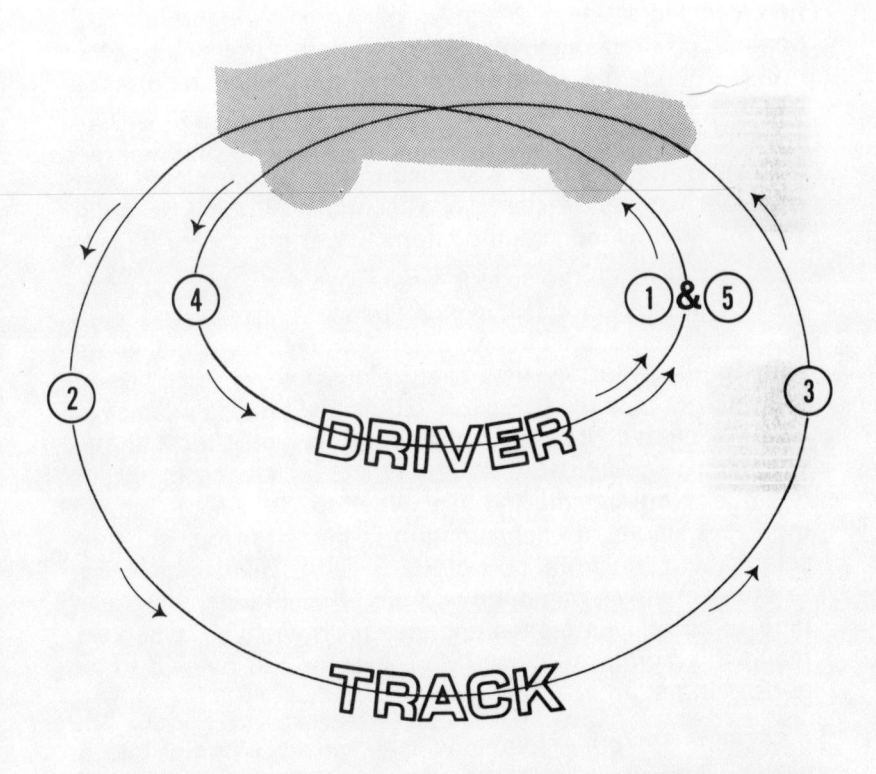

In the above illustration, we are looking at a closed loop system. The driver (1) produces an input into the car. The car then reacts (2) on a track surface. As this action takes place, the track then responds (3) with reference to our vehicle. The vehicle then reacts under our driver (4), and if the original action was not totally correct, the driver (5) then feeds in corrective action and we begin the process again.

The closer we can come to an automatic run, the faster we become. Each decision our subconscious mind makes causes our body to respond and correctly move the car. Thus more time can be spent consciously evaluation and fine tuning our run.

In any closed loop system, in order to understand ultimate value we must examine the weakest link. In an average car-driver system, a driver is the strongest part, with our vehicle being the weakest link at low speeds. As the speed increases, at some point car and driver are equal. At high speeds, a driver becomes the weakest point. At ultra high speeds, reaction time of the driver, then subsequent mechanical correction, actually adds to the severity of a situation, rather than hoped/for corrective action. The next time you hear a driver tell you how he corrected a skid at 200 miles per hour in his formula car, don't laugh in his face, but don't get ready to go practice the move. Nobody has reflexes fast enough actually to correct a 200 mile per hour skid. True, a driver is attempting to correct his skid, but when reaction time of a man like Andretti is not more than two tenths of a second quick, his car moves over sixty feet in those two tenths of a second at 200 miles per hour. You tell us how much can be done under those conditions!

Let's examine the speeds where you can affect your car. We go through four basic moves when we cause our car to go in a certain direction. First we must identify the fact that we are coming to a pylon. We then analyze possible routes to take in order to get past the pylon in the quickest time, then analyze what we might do if we are somewhat incorrect. After analysis, We reach a decision as to which route to travel, and finally our head tells our hands and feet what to do. As our speed increases, more of each function is placed in our subconscious mind, and fewer conscious decisions need to be made. At some point we can operate a car efficiently and still have time to correct unforseen changes in the vehicle. When we reach this point, the closed loop system can be said to be performing at an optimum level.

There are other functions that can be plugged into a system, and with time, more and more functions become subconscious reactions, or conditioned reflexes.

Mentally, we have four basic levels of consciousness. The bottom level is an unconscious incompetent. This is a state of mind where the individual has no idea or knowledge about a given subject, and therefore operates in a highly inefficient manner.

The second level of consciousness is a conscious incompetent. In this state of mind, a person is aware he has too little knowledge about a subject to operate efficiently, and seeks additional knowledge and understanding.

The third level comprises a conscious competent. This person can operate efficiently on a conscious level. Most drivers fit in the second or third level when they begin to autocross. Unfortunately, few people ever get above the third level. We say unfortunately, but in reality, it's a good thing, because the fourth level, unconscious competent, is where winners are. As cruel as it may seem, the fewer winners we have to compete with, the more trophies we take home. In our opinion, 95% of all winners fit in this category, and the other 5% are kidding themselves.

An unconscious competent is a person who has worked long and hard on programming his or her mind to accept a conditioned reflex reaction level of mental and physical being. These are drivers who, when asked why they are so good, smile and claim not to know. In reality, they are saying, "If you have to ask how, you probably don't have enough perseverance to reach an unconscious competent level".

Also part of a closed loop system is the psychology of winning. If every time you approach a given track layout you say, "I can win at any track, except X", you're probably right. If in your mind, track X is going to beat you, indeed it will.

Many people have asked what we think about during an event. We have to answer this question with qualifications. First of all, we think about our students and their cars. We've both been involved for long enough that we don't get too concerned over our own runs until our class is up. One reason is that when our car pulls in, we're ready to run. We don't play the game of get to a track, then set up our cars.

Secondly, we walk the course very carefully, usually more than once. After we have done this, we watch other cars run, and watch for patterns to form at a given pylon, or certain sections of the track. We watch our students, and offer advice as we see improper moves, or may suggest an alternative that is easy to see from outside a car, but more difficult from inside. Very few autocrossers are complete loners. Talk to friends who are running in a different class. Take turns observing each other's runs.

One of the most important 'games' to play with your competition is to keep them guessing. We have done such things as writing numbers on the side of a tire that vaguely

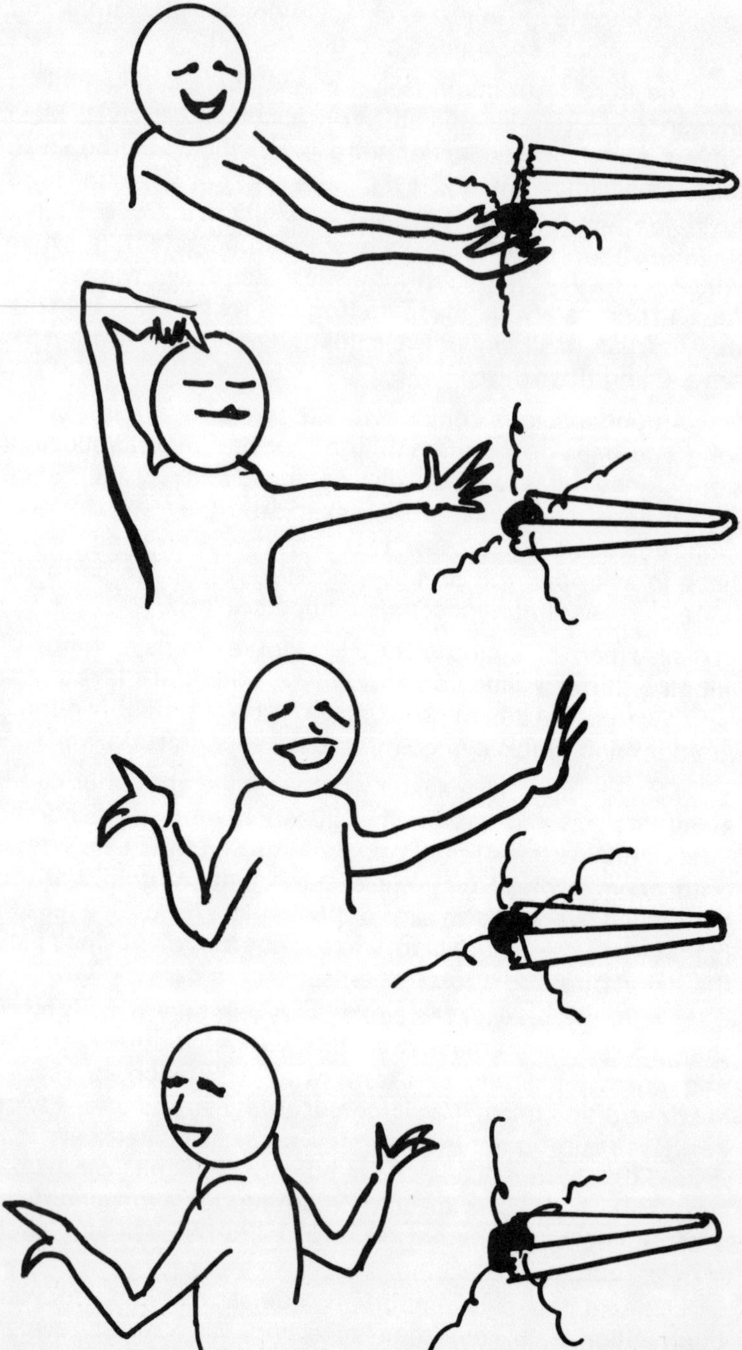

Levels of consciousness are a vital part of the closed loop system. Let's set the scene. A person is holding a piece of charcoal with a pair of tongs. The charcoal is gray in color. As the holder approaches the various levels of consciousness regarding charcoal, let's see the reaction of the four recipients!

Question: "How would you like a nice piece of charcoal?"
Answer from the unconscious incompetent: "Wow, is it free? I never turn down anything free. Sure, give it here."

Obviously the recipient has no knowledge about charcoal, and will get burned.

Question: "How would you like a nice piece of charcoal?"
Answer from the conscious incompetent: "Uhh, let's see, charcoal - - - don't think so. Somebody told me something about charcoal. I don't remember just what it was, but think it had something to do with the color. No, think I'll pass."

The recipient does not really know about charcoal, but declines the offer due to limited knowledge learned at an earlier date. He passes somewhat reluctantly, but nonetheless turns down the gift.

Question: "How would you like a nice piece of charcoal?"
Answer from the conscious competent: "No thanks. I can see by the color the charcoal is burning. This is confirmed in my mind by the fact that you are holding the gray charcoal with a pair of tongs. In addition, I have nothing to carry a piece of hot charcoal in, and even if I did, by the time I got home it would have burned out. Thank you for the offer though."

Question: "How would you like a nice piece of charcoal?"
Answer from the unconscious competent: "You must be kidding. What in the world would I do with that?"

This person obviously knows the same facts as the conscious competent, but has them programmed and instantly analyzes the options. As a result, the decision is rapid, and definitive.

Where do you fit in these illustrations? Look honestly at your driving ability, then practice until you reach at least the third level. Remember, practice makes perfect, but only when the right moves are practiced.

emble a possible tire pressure. If somebody asks if it is tire pressure, we say, "No, it's just some numbers we wrote on here." We have told the truth, but our competiton may make an air pressure change that will give us a winning edge.

Always stand, walk, and talk like a winner, but don't be cocky. Nobody likes a smart alec, but everybody loves a winner. Offer suggestions when asked, but at the same time remember that competition is competition. We will never suggest a setup that is wrong. If it is a competitor in our class, we try to deal only in generalities, unless it's a student of ours. In a recent autocross, Dick was beaten by a student. It was the greatest defeat he has ever had. If there were any possible way for us to put winning psychology in your head with this book, then have you beat us in heads-up competition, we have accomplished our ultimate goal. It's more fun to run with a select group of winners, than all the losers in the world.

When you belt yourself in a car and strap on your helmet, forget the outside world. Nothing should be going through your mind but the run itself. What your competitor has done, or will do, is his concern, not yours. Above all else, forget about the clock in terms of a certain time. A driver who says, "I'm going to run a 1:04.832 this time" is only headed for a disappointment. Run your car to the best of your ability, and your car's capability, and you have done your job. If you do everything right and still lose, you have been beaten. At that point, you need to search inside your head, and in your car, to come up with a faster combination. After all, isn't that what competition is all about?

Trailing Accelerator, Trailing Brake, and Torque Lag

Trailing is defined in the dictionary as "to drag or let drag behind one, or, to diminish and dwindle, as a sound." When we apply trailing to acceleration and braking, it is exactly as the dictionary definition says.

With a trailing accelerator, acceleration is trailing off as braking action is increasing. In the case of trailing brake, braking action is trailing off as acceleration is increasing.

Let's look at a scale of zero-to-ten for both accelerating, and braking. When we are at ten on the acceleration scale, we are at zero on the braking scale. As we wish to slow down, we go from ten to nine on acceleration, and from zero to one on braking force. Acceleration then drops to eight and braking increases to two. At any point on the scale, if you add the two components together, the total will always be ten. This rise and fall actually takes place in much less than one second.

As an example, we are going to practice in a straight line. The first exercise will be to set up a pylon where you have room enough to accelerate to twenty miles per hour, brake to zero, and have room enough for error. Accelerate to twenty, then put your car in neutral. Apply a braking force with your left foot that you think will stop your car at the pylon. Do not change pressure once you have started to brake. Let your car come to a complete stop. This doesn't mean ½ mph, this means zero mph. This is the toughest thing to convince our students of. If your car is rolling at all, the whole exercise is blown.

If you stopped before reaching the pylon, do it again and apply slightly less pressure. If you rolled past the pylon before

```
10  +   0
 9  +   1
 8  +   2
 7  +   3
 6  +   4
 5  +   5   } =10
 4  +   6
 3  +   7
 2  +   8
 1  +   9
 0  +  10
```

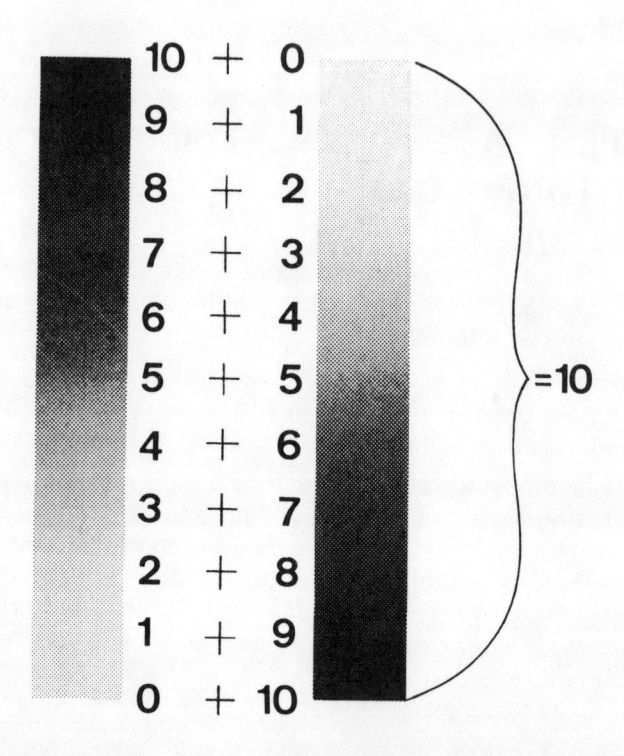

By thinking about a scale for accelerating, and an equal and opposite scale for braking, we can better understand trailing brake and trailing accelerator. As you approach a corner under full acceleration, your acceleration scale would read ten, while your braking scale would read zero. As you begin deceleration with your throttle, you are beginning to brake. In the short time frame while you are applying full braking, you are releasing your acceleration at the same rate. At any point along the scale, the combination of braking and acceleration will equal ten. Likewise, as you pull off a corner, your braking will drop from ten back to zero as your acceleration travels from zero to ten.

stopping, next time apply slightly more pressure. Do this exercise enough that you can be driving, apply one pressure, and stop the car where you desire.

Next, try the same basic move, but during the last two or three feet of roll, lift your foot slightly off the brake. This will cause the car to stop without rocking as your suspension finally comes to rest. We have dissipated the rolling energy in a smooth manner. If you do not feel a difference, perhaps you did not come to a complete stop in the previous exercise. By practicing this move, you will be able to make minute adjustments in braking pressure without upsetting the balance of your car.

Now, give yourself enough room to reach thirty, slow to ten, then accelerate back to thirty. Accelerate to thirty mph. As you reach the point where you wish to brake, start to apply braking pressure with your left foot, and at the same time, lift your right foot slowly off the accelerator. Increase your braking pressure to reach ten miles per hour at the pylon. As you pass the pylon at ten mph, reapply accelerator pressure, and start releasing braking pressure. Remember the ten score. Too much accelerator trailing as you attempt to slow down will cause you to overshoot the objective. Likewise, too much trailing brake will cause a loss of accleration.

Now that we can do it in a straight line, let's practice on a corner. The key is to know how to brake at the point of incipient skid or maximum braking effort of your vehicle/tire/surface combination. Likewise, when we accelerate off the corner, we want to have our car pull as hard as possible without producing excessive wheel spin.

Another factor is torque lag of our drive train. There is a momentary delay as the suspension unwinds upon deceleration, and winds up during acceleration. Each car will have a slightly different delay factor, and only practice will teach you just how much wind or unwind your car has.

The reasons why we use a trailing system are many. Let's examine a few. First of all, when we approach a corner, we need to scrub off approximately ninety percent of our straightaway speed in a straight line. Our brakes, if compared to engine power, are very strong.

As an example, the average car with 200 horsepower has a braking equivalent of over 600 horsepower. This means we can stop much faster than we can accelerate. With such being the case, we want to preserve speed produced by our engine as far into a corner as possible.

Pure logic tells us a car can stop better with all four tires planted squarely on the ground than it can off balance. If our engine pulls two drive wheels, but brakes work on all four, any form of logic tells us we can slow quicker than we can go. If we attempt to apply braking effort and turn at the same time, at least one wheel, the rear inside, will be very light on the road surface. Since all four wheels will have equal braking pressure applied by our braking system, the light wheel probably will slide. When this happens, our other three wheels do not have enough adhesive ability to pick up traction lost by one. Again, logic tells us three tire patches cannot support as much force as four. The end result is a spin, or a very off-balance turn.

By using a trailing brake, maximum pressure is being applied in a straight line, then being reduced in a corner, yet we still have braking effort in the turn. Slip angle creates braking forces. Thus, a tighter turn produces more braking as long as we keep our drift not more than approximately 20 degrees.

As this is taking place, our suspension components are being squeezed by the pitch motion of our car. By trailing the braking effort, components are allowed to move more slowly, and remain in balance, rather than loading and unloading under various rates of acceleration and deceleration.

When autocrossing, the name of the game is to get from point "A" to point "B" as quickly as possible. Since the use of a trailing brake theory can get us through a corner at a higher overall average speed, this is in itself reason enough to employ the principle.

With high horsepower cars, trailing accelerator allows us to run deeper into a turn, then utilize maximum braking effort at the last thousandth of a second. As we come off the turn, trailing brake and a smooth foot on the accelerator once again play an important role. As you apply accelerator or brake pedal pressure, think about curling your toes over the pedal. This will give you closer physical tolerance and will sharpen your run.

Let's assume we have negotiated a tight first gear turn, and are about to enter a slalom. If we jump on our accelerator, the rear wheels begin to spin. At what position from the idle position to the floor did pedal pressure allow enough fuel into our engine to make the rear end break loose? We really have no idea. If we were to squeeze the accelerator, as soon as the rear wheels begin to spin, we know by releasing just a small amount of pressure from the accelerator we will regain traction, and our car will again pull at maximum.

There is a slight fallacy in this statement. In reality, your car is still accelerating when it begins to spin, so therefore the point at which you will regain traction is slightly higher in rpm's than our example.

If your car is in the medium horsepower range and begins to spin, ease up very slightly and feel your rear tires "catch up" with the power curve of your engine. As soon as traction is regained, continue a downward stroke of your foot on the accelerator. A general rule is that as horsepower decreases, the car is more forgiving. This is not to say that a driver of less talent can win in a low horsepower car. In fact, it takes every bit as much ability to drive a low horsepower car, and in some cases more.

Concentrate on squeezing both the accelerator and brake. Once you have mastered this combination, and add it to proper use of your hands, you are on your way to becoming a winner.

Learn to squeeze your brakes, not punch them. In our illustration, the chick doesn't want to be clobbered. Think about an egg under your foot every time you apply your brakes. As you wish to push down on your pedal, remember the egg. Just as the egg contains a chick, so do our brakes contain the key to contact with the track surface. If we fight with the track, it will break our adhesion limit as easily as we can break the egg.

Types of Corners

In autocrossing, or for that matter any form of driving, there are four basic types of corners to contend with. No two corners are alike, and thus cannot be driven in exactly the same manner. However, once your learn the characteristics of a given type corner, you can negotiate nearly any turn fitting this general description with knowledge and understanding.

Ingress

An ingress corner is a turn at the end of a straightaway. In autocrossing, this is an important corner, since we have sufficient speed to hit pylons if we run too deep, or too close to pylons marking the corner, before braking. Since we have established that we can stop our car faster than we can accelerate, we need to keep power on as long as possible in every straightaway. As we approach a turn, wait as long as possible to apply your brakes. At the precise moment of braking, apply your brakes one tenth of a second prior to releasing your accelerator. By making this move, your suspension will not have a bounce, or rebound, as it goes from a 'nose high' position to a 'nose down' position. Watch a driver who uses his right foot for both the accelerator and brake, but does not attempt any sort of heel and toe routine or left foot braking. His car will nose dive, then bounce at least once before settling down under braking strain. By braking as we suggest, you will save bounce time and spend more time actually slowing down, rather than bouncing your suspension and changing the shape of your tire patch on the track surface.

As you approach each corner, think in terms of scrubbing off 90% of your excess speed. As you begin to turn, pick your

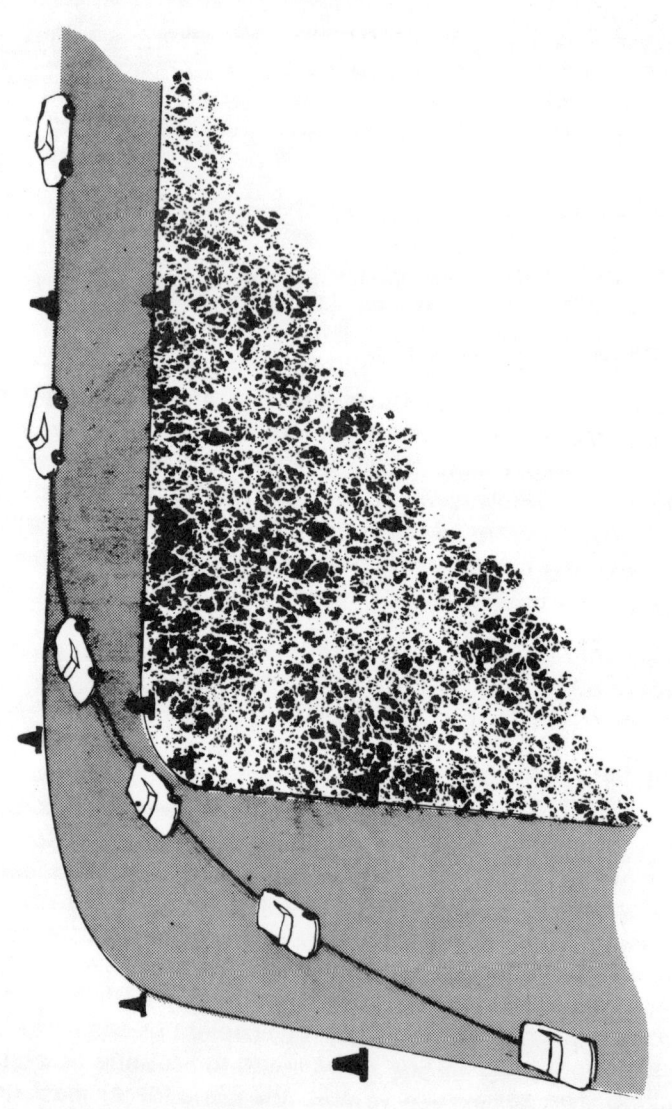

An ingress corner allows us to maintain acceleration longer, then a trailing accelerator, and heavy braking get the car slowed for a proper line. As we cross the apex and begin acceleration, we move to the outside edge of our pylons. Maintain smooth power and keep your car balanced for the next corner as you trail your brakes.

foot slightly off the brake pedal to keep your inside rear tire from sliding. As you trail off the braking effort, begin to squeeze power back on. As you try to add power, think of curling your toes around the accelerator, rather than pushing on the pedal. The same rule applies here as when we entered the corner. Apply your accelerator one tenth of a second before you release total braking effort. This has just the opposite effect as entering a corner. In other words, at this point, we want to keep the nose down, thus keeping good road contact at our front tires.

As you enter the ingress corner, don't forget the slip angle of your front tires as a braking force. The tighter a turn, the more braking effort you will have from steering action.

If as you enter a corner your car begins to drift, or skid, you will "turn in the direction of the slide." Try thinking of this action in another term, and you can improve communication between your car, and your mind. "Keep your front wheels going in the desired direction of travel."

If we examine a skid, slide, or power slide, we will find in all three cases your front wheels are placed in the desired direction of travel to correct a slide. Too many people crank in more steering effort than is required, and only aid a slide by moving their tire patch past maximum adhesion levels.

Egress

An egress turn leads onto a straightaway. Since the object is to be going as fast as possible on all straight sections, we want to pull off each corner with maximum speed as we run down the chute.

With this turn, we brake earlier. In fact, 95% of our braking effort will take place before we move from the extreme outside edge of the racing surface toward the apex, or a point more than one half the measured distance through a turn. By scrubbing off an extra 5% of our speed, we can keep the car in close, hit a late apex, and allow more rapid acceleration as we come off the turn.

As you come off a turn into the straight section, those of you with super strong cars will experience oversteer tendencies. The best way to eliminate this is to let your car pull as straight as possible toward the extreme outside of the surface turning very slowly toward the straightaway. As your speed in any gear increases, the ability of your engine to spin the rear tires decreases. Thus, the more slowly you can turn under heavy acceleration the faster you can run down the straight.

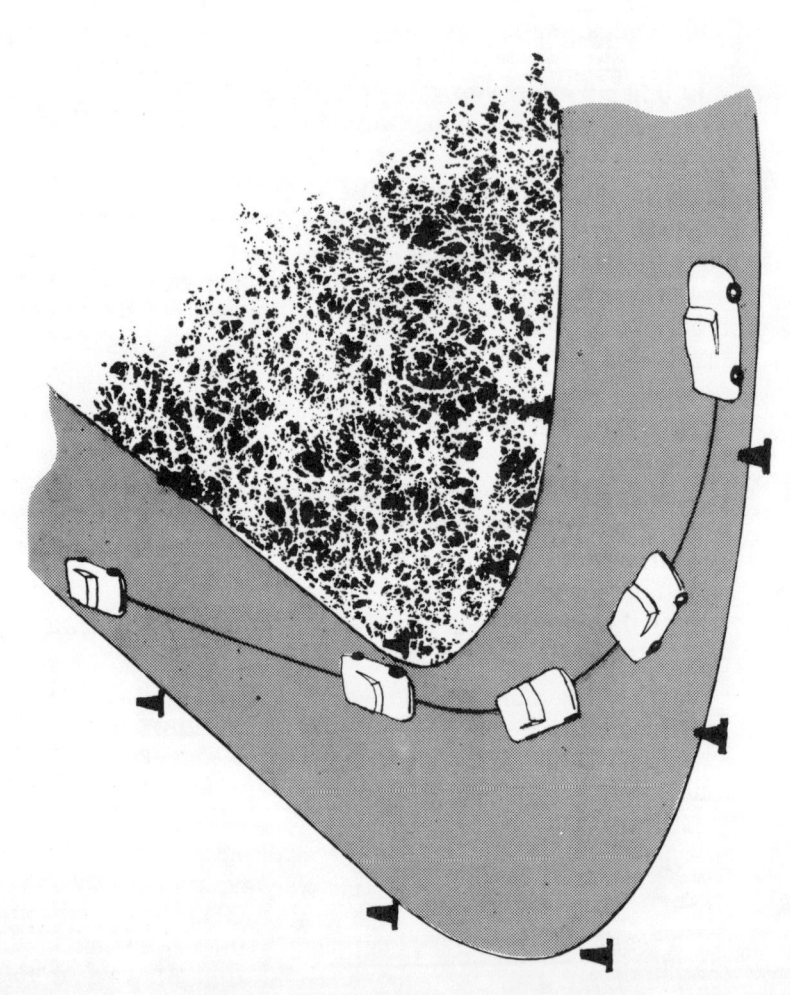

When driving an egress corner it is important to brake early, take an earlier apex than you will for the ingress corner, then apply power as early as possible for a rapid exit onto the straightaway.

Be careful not to pull a shift to the next higher gear just as you come off a corner. When you make your shift, the driveline allows your car to 'sag,' or relax. This causes suspension overloading momentarily on the outside of your car, then as your tire compression rebounds you apply power, and away you go, spinning and wondering what happened.

We can't say enough about keeping a suspension compressed by either constant acceleration or constant braking. Just as we use shock absorbers to dampen springs, we use proper control of our feet on the pedals to dampen our entire machine. Failure to do so puts us in virtually the same category as an old worn out race car with a 'loosie goosie' suspension.

Neutral

A neutral corner can best be defined as 'a corner with a constant arc of more than 160 degrees.' This type of corner is often referred to as a sweeper. It is one of the most frustrating type of corners, because when you are doing everything right, it feels like you aren't really doing anything.

The key to a neutral corner is to find a maximum speed at which you can get from entry to exit, then be satisfied with riding it out. With modern tires, as we previously mentioned, the upper limit of adhesion has such a close tolerance that an increase of one or two miles per hour can make the difference between staying on a corner and plowing a corn field. We learned a long time ago that J. B. and Dick vs. Farmall and John Deere could not be a compatible combination. We made a deal that briefly states, we wouldn't plow fields if they wouldn't enter solo events. The arrangement has worked fine to date, and we intend to try and keep peace.

A neutral corner looks quite innocent to an observer, but may be a bear to drive. Don't attempt to go too quickly in this type of turn. Remember, you cannot gain time in an autocross, you can only preserve or lose time. The neutral corner can preserve time, but if you push too hard, it can lose a bunch!

Esses

Esses also are somewhat frustrating to drive, because they tend to do almost the same number on your head as a neutral corner. As with all types of turns, there are various forms of esses, but they all have a common trait, they can cost a bunch of time if you try to go too fast. A slalom is an example of ess turns. A well laid out course will usually have single pylons placed at uneven distances. If you don't read these distances

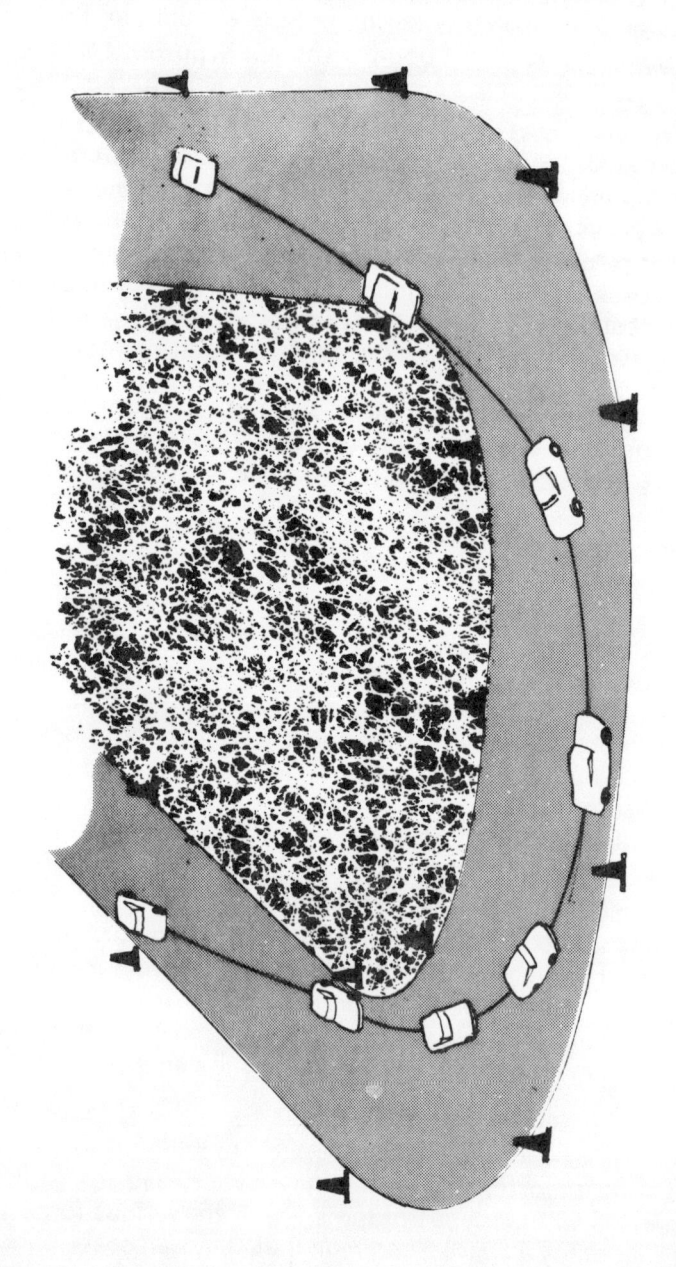

In a neutral corner don't get excited and think you need to do more driving. Settle down, allow the car to run at the upper adhesion limits of your tires, and stay smooth.

properly, you will either be going too fast and look like the pendulum on a grandfather clock, or you won't have sufficient speed to get a quick time. Once you have learned your car's adhesion limit, don't attempt to go past it.

With many slaloms, how you get into the first corner can set the stage for your entire run. If you negotiate the first pylon too fast, then try to slow down, there is a good chance of losing control before pylon number two has gone by. Take the first pylon in a manner as you would the ingress corner, then switch your style as though you had entered a neutral corner. From the first pylon, to the last, evaluate each distance, then decide where each arc fits a category. This evaluation is done before an event starts, as you walk the course. If you should happen to run an event where walking the course is not mandatory, do it anyway. The theory of scoping out a course on your first run so you can run fast on your next two or three is the difference between winning and watching. Make every run count, not just the last two.

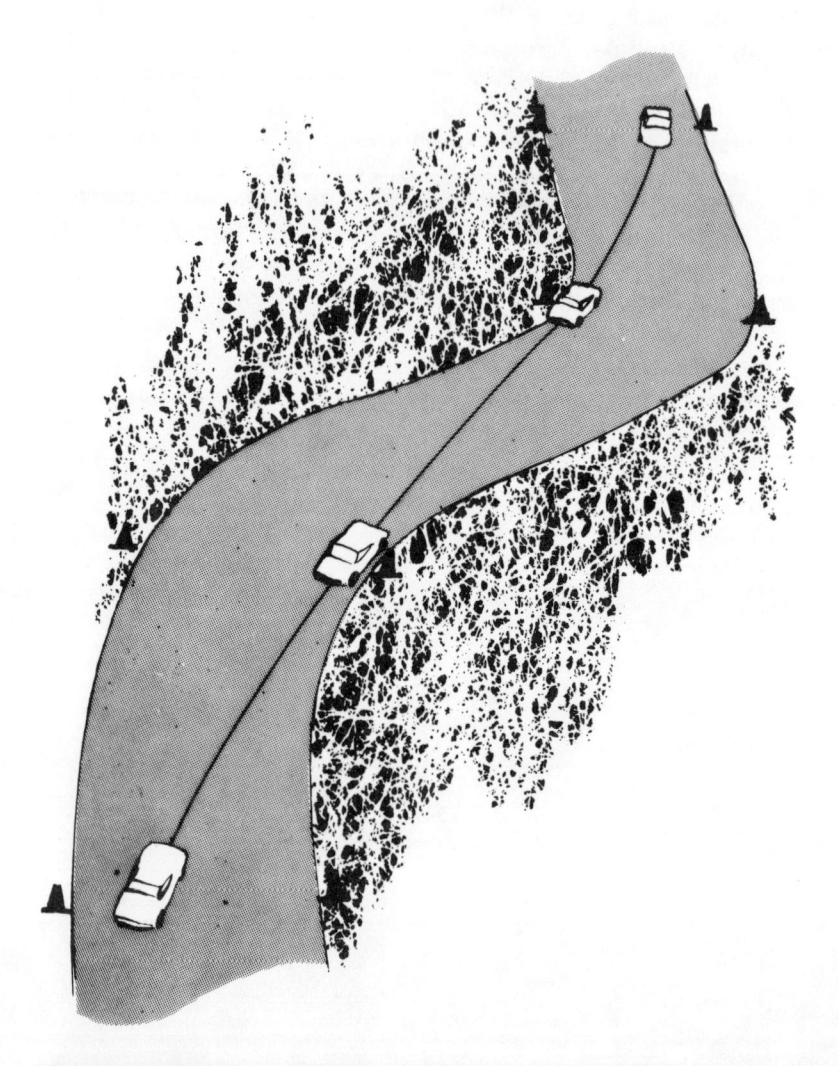

Esses are somewhat frustrating and should be driven carefully. Too much power will only result in a momentary loss of control. As with the neutral corner, there is a maximum speed your car can travel. Above the limit you will only lose time by trying harder.

Cornering and Tire Pressure Guidelines

Let's examine a corner, and remove it from our four categories. What we mean is this — examine the corner as if it came from nowhere, and leads nowhere.

On an average course, there are very few boundaries saying 'you can't go here'. As a result, driving in solo competition can, in many ways be more difficult than driving on a race track. On a track you have limits within which to work. If you exceed this limit, you are fighting with the Farmall man! On a solo course, you must learn to establish mental limits within which to operate.

Any car is capable of tracking in three positions relative to the road surface. These three positions are neutral steer, understeer, and oversteer. If we examine the net result of a turning arc, rather than just the front wheels, we can better understand what these positions are, and how we can affect them.

Neutral Steer

Neutral steer is when your car can corner under power and will hold a given set in the corner once the slip angle is established. A neutral steer car is most advantageous to have for a proficient driver. By properly aligning the car in a corner, or upon entry, you will always have reserve steering capability left with either the steering wheel, accelerator or brake combination. On a diagram, the center of gravity would be half way from front to rear.

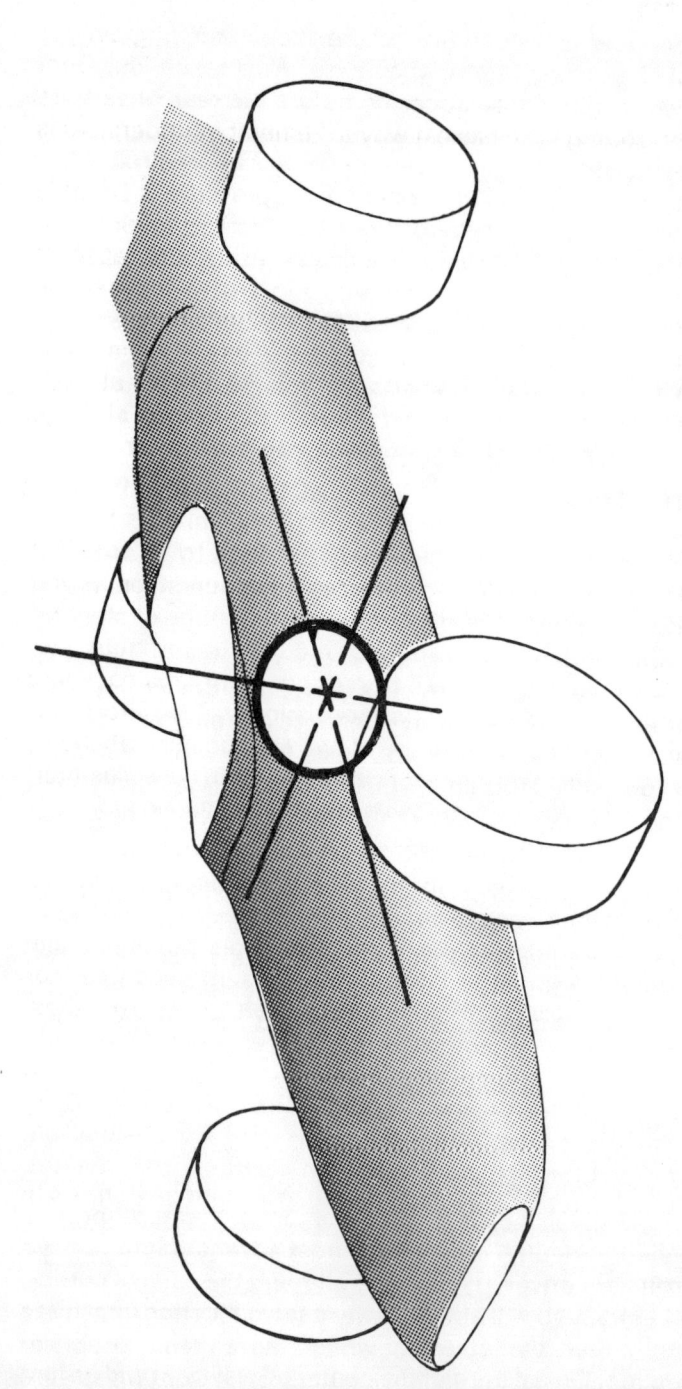

If the center of gravity of a vehicle is located exactly in the vehicle's center, the car will be neutral steering if all four tires are of equal size and pressure.

Understeer

Understeer is a condition where the center of gravity is ahead of the center of our wheelbase. As a result, our front wheels will begin to lose adhesion before the rear wheels are subject to sliding. The easiest way to remember understeer is that the traveled arc is 'under,' or less than desired. Most American built cars will understeer if tire pressure is equal in all four tires. The best method of correcting this situation is to ease off your accelerator slightly, or if you are braking, ease off the brakes. By doing this, the slip angle of a tire can be effectively increased, and more tractive forces can be exerted on the track surface. As you ease off the gas, you can also crank in a little more steering effort. If you are already at a slip angle of 20° or more, you can reduce your steering arc slightly, pick up tractive force, then turn back into the corner.

A maneuver that can be used on many Porsche automobiles points out an increase of tractive force as the slip angle decreases from approximately 23° back to 19 or 20°. If you are in a corner, and have considerable understeer, as you are ready to come out of the corner, begin your exit steering motion approximately one half second before you think you should. By so doing, you will bring your front tires back into and through the maximum slip angle of high tractive effort, and your car will feel like the front end has aligned itself ahead of the rear end, rather than the opposite. After you have mastered this technique, you can run with more room for error.

As a general rule, you will increase cornering power on an autocross car by increasing tire pressure. The fallacy in this statement is when you are already overinflated, then add more air. As you add or take out air in your front tires, remember that the net effect is going to take all four tires into account. For example, by removing three pounds of air from the front tires, you have effectively increased the net resulting pressure in your rear tires. By experimenting with tire pressures, you can probably do more for your handling than any other tuning within the same time frame. Another factor to consider is a camber change which is caused in an x pattern from rear tire pressures. Increasing or decreasing the right rear tire will affect your left front camber angle.

Oversteer

Oversteer is a condition where the center of gravity is behind the center of your wheelbase. As a result, your rear wheels will begin to lose adhesion before the front wheels are subject to sliding. The easiest way to remember oversteer, is

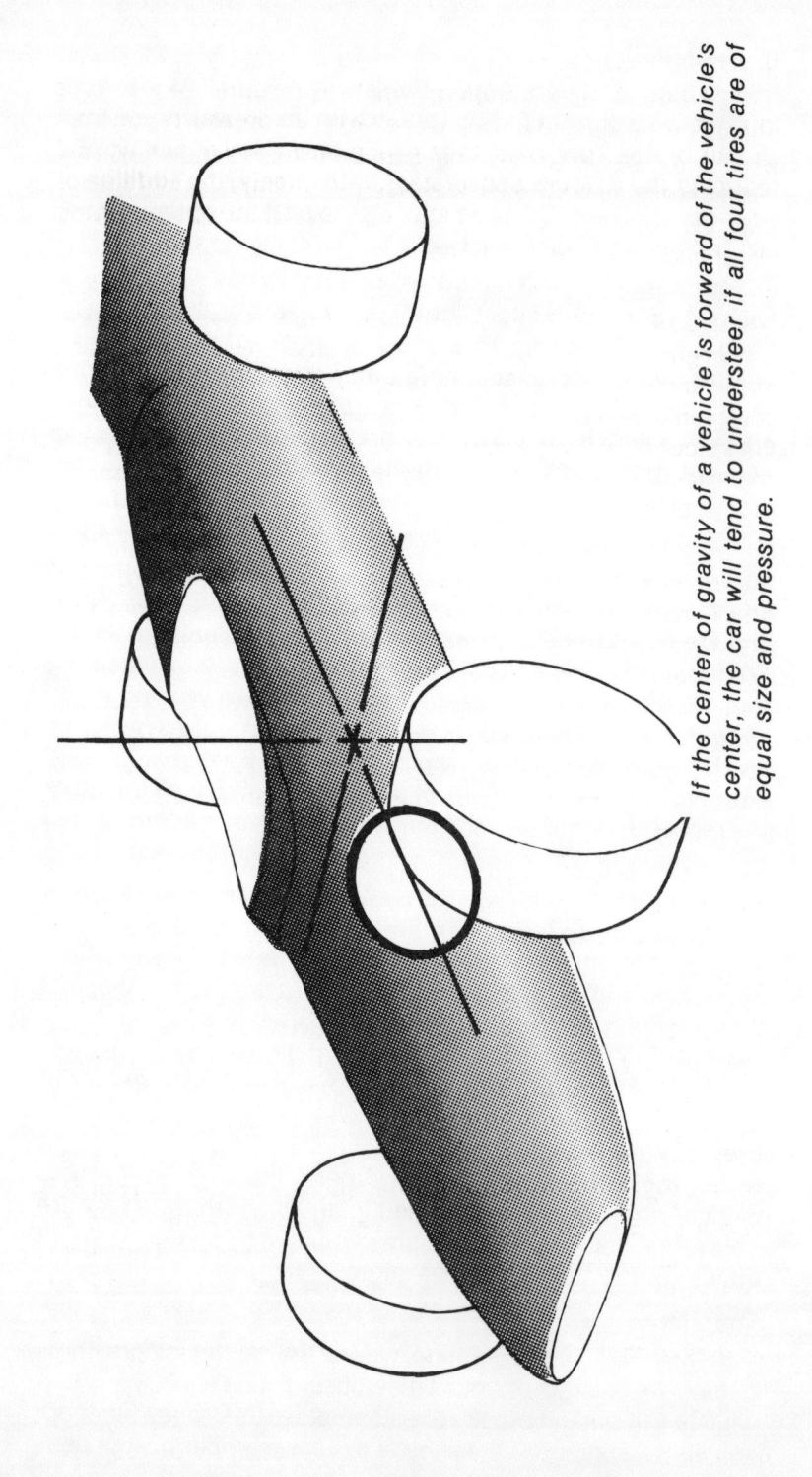

If the center of gravity of a vehicle is forward of the vehicle's center, the car will tend to understeer if all four tires are of equal size and pressure.

that the traveled arc is 'over,' or more than desired. Most rear engine cars tend to oversteer if the tire pressure is equal in all four tires. To correct this condition with air pressure, you take air out of the front tires, thus giving less tractive ability, and reducing the amount of oversteer. Conversely, the addition of air in the rear tires will give better adhesion if the optimum limit has not already been reached.

To reduce oversteer by driving, let's start an oversteer condition by cranking steering input into our car. As our rear end begins to come around, we must steer toward the outside of the arc, into the slide, or as previously mentioned, around a corner in the direction of travel. By setting our car for a corner, then steering with the slide, we can improve our control point and overall speed in the corner. It can be safely said that an oversteering car is by far the hardest to control in an autocross.

We can add some general rules to go by with regard to air pressure, but each car is different, so you will have to experiment to know what is best for your car. In general, for an understeering car, add our 4 or 5 pounds more pressure to your front tires. For an oversteering car, set your tires just the opposite. If you happen to live in Eutopia and your car is neutral, then tune the setup by adding and subtracting equal amounts of air until the maximum cornering force is generated.

The best way to test steering characteristics is to run on a test circle, but since most of us do not have our own track, other methods are adequate.

Pick a deserted parking lot, or road with little traffic. Drive through a corner with a constant radius at a speed where you will not slide. Now, increase your speed in small increments until you begin to slide. If the front wheels start to slide first, you have an understeer condition. Add 5 pounds of air to your front tires and try again. Keep adjusting air pressure until your car feels neutral. Note the tire pressure immediately after reaching what you feel is optimum, then go home. Let your car sit still until the tires have completely cooled to ambient, or outside air temperature, and measure the amount of pressure with cold tires. 'Cold' tires are whatever the outside air temperature is, or a simpler way of saying the same thing is the air temperature in your tires after the car has not been driven for an hour or more.

If the rear tires start to lose adhesion in your testing, you have an oversteer condition. Add 5 pounds of air to your rear

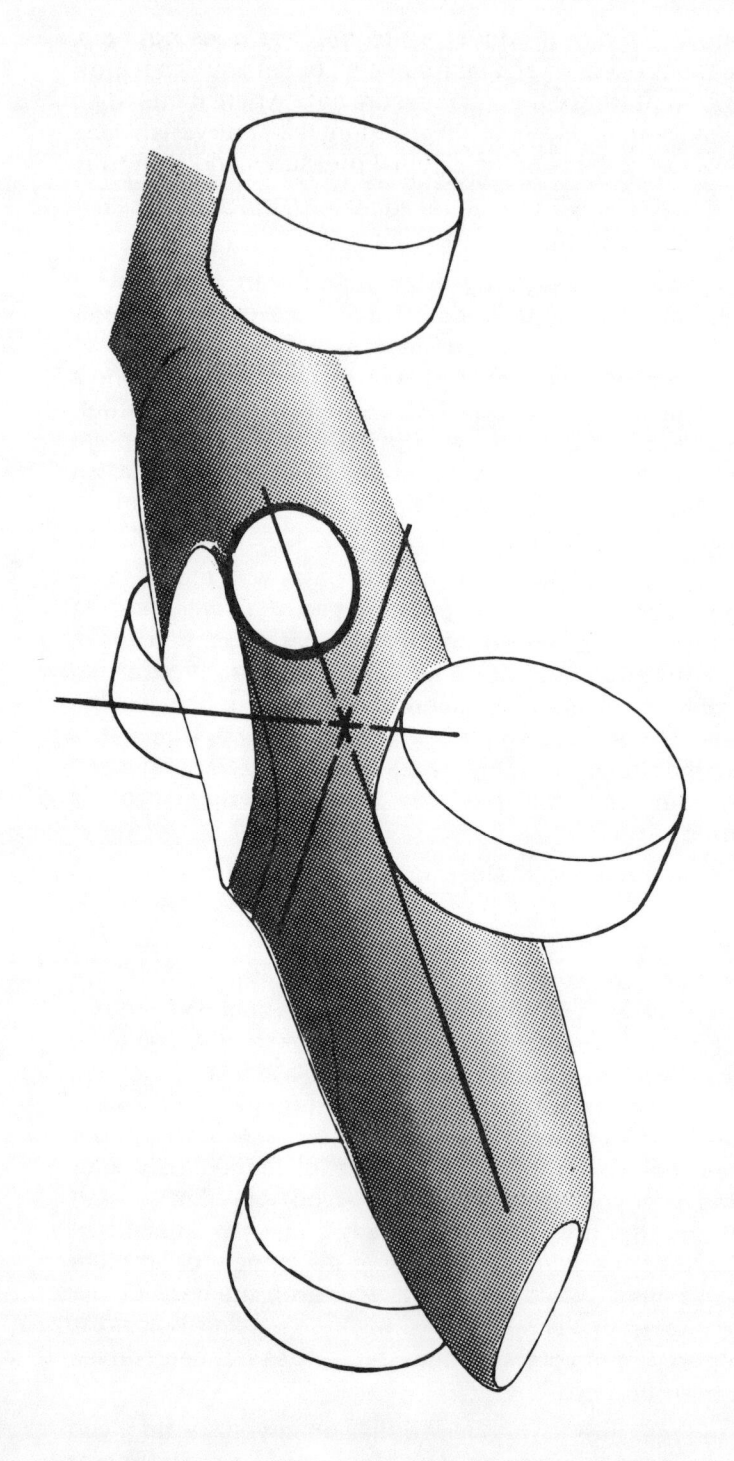

If the center of gravity of a vehicle is behind the vehicle's center, the car will tend to oversteer if all four tires are of equal size and pressure.

tires and try again. If adding air to the rear does not help, reverse the procedure and take some air out of your front tires. Do this after putting your rear pressure back where it was when you began testing. Never try to test more than one variable at a time. Always go back to the original pressures and start from there.

Time Ranking

As we walk a course, it is important to decide where the fast sections, slow sections, and neutral sections are. Usually a layout will be divided into these three groupings.

Our priority will depend on the type of car we are driving. If we have a low powered car, slower sections will rank first, since our forte' will be handling, not power. If we are driving a strong car, perhaps faster sections of the course will rank number one. The fallacy, of course, is the car that does everything well. In this case, we will have to revert back to our ability to drive a certain type of corner. If we are very good at slaloms, be sure to get set up properly in the first gate, and make time count in this section.

Corners can generally be ranked with the egress corner first. Since we win by running the fastest time, it stands to reason that each turn leading out onto a straightaway will rank on top.

Second priority should go to the ingress corner, since we want to hold our speed as long as possible at the end of a straightaway.

Third priority has to go to a neutral corner, since a mistake here will cause a great loss of time. The frustration factor can lead us into the trap of Murphy's Law, which basically states that if something can go wrong, it will. Do not allow yourself to become upset at a neutral corner.

Last on our list are esses. Since these critters are somewhat like the neutral corner, but usually require more driver attention, they are not quite as critical. A busy driver is usually an attentive driver. There are people who will disagree

Corner Priorities
1. **Egress**
2. **Ingress**
3. **Neutral**
4. **Esses**

Corner priorities are an important factor during an event. Proper corner classification lets us know where we can save the most time, and where we need to be cautious. Top priority should go to the egress corner since we need maximum speed on a straightaway. If we set up for a proper exit, we enter the straight at a higher speed.

Second in rank is the ingress turn. We need to hold our straightaway speed as long as possible, apply our brakes efficiently, and set up for the corner.

Neutral corners, and esses can be swapped in priority depending on your ability to drive each type. We prefer to rank neutral corners third since they require more thought and concentration. It is easy to get lulled into a false sense of security in a neutral corner. With esses, we know there will be a turning input required. Therefore, we are forced to think more about esses. This tends to make them less apt to be forgotten, or taken for granted.

with these last two priorities. Our best advice is to evaluate your performance with these two types of corners, and give them whichever priority they earn.

One common error we see constantly is a driver who makes a mistake, and is going to drive harder to make up for it. If you fit in this category, you probably do not win many events. You should always be driving at the upper safe limit. To surpass a safe run will only cost more pylons, and more time. Once you have goofed, forget it. No matter how long you look in the mirror, the pylon will not set itself back up, so why stare at past history?

Rudyard Kipling once said, "There are only two things in this life of value, that which concerns you, and that which does not. Be concerned only with that which concerns you." His point should be well taken in the world of motorsport. We can only control a certain number of factors. Once a situation is beyond our control, there is no valid reason for concern.

Reading A Racing Surface

Since solo events are often held in parking lots or on airport taxiways, not all surfaces are alike. We need to understand what the composition is, and how we can change our car to best handle each surface.

Concrete is most often found on an airport track. To be technically correct, this type surface is Portland Cement Concrete. It consists of sand, gravel, and cement. The exact mixture depends on the desired pounds per square inch of strength called for in the specifications when the surface was built. Higher ratings contain more cement in the mixture. The most used surface is a brushed finish. This finish gives the greatest amount of traction. One thing to watch for is an old concrete surface that may scrub off under pressures of an event, or a surface that has been raced on for many years, and has become polished. Traction limits may be greatly reduced. Don't be fooled by concrete — it isn't all the same.

Since concrete gives the best bite, tire pressures may need to be slightly higher to keep your tires from rolling into the sidewall under heavy cornering stress.

The most widely used surface for autocrossing is asphalt, or asphaltic concrete. This surface is prepared by mixing liquid asphalt, a petroleum product, sand, and gravel. The exact surface depends on the particular blend of these three components.

New asphalt does not have high gripping ability, as does slightly aged asphalt. As the surface oxidizes, it becomes somewhat more adhesive. Our prime concern with the sticking ability of asphalt is the gravel size, and type of sand used. A coarse sand, and crushed rock or sea shells make the best surface for roadholding. In many parts of the country, river run rock or gravel is used. This is gravel that has been washed along in a river. Thus, surfaces are smoother, and do not grip tires as well.

As a general rule, you can run slightly less air pressure on river run asphalt due to a lower gripping ability. Two or three pounds less air will usually get the job done. It should be remembered that each surface is different, and will require setup changes. The smart autocrosser keeps a diary of what worked best at each event.

Your diary should contain the weather conditions, track temperature, (this can be taken with an inexpensive meat thermometer), track surface type, tire pressure, any changes you make during an event, and any other information you might feel is important. The list can get quite lengthy if you let it. We like to keep track of tread depth, and brand or type of tire for each situation.

There have been many arguments about the best brand of tire, most accurate air gauge, or best pyrometer. If you keep one basic fact in mind, all others will tend to remain constant. If you learn to run successfully on a given tire, and are winning, why change? If your tire gauge reads three pounds higher than another competitors, so what? Learn what your gauge says, and stick with it. What difference does it actually make if you think you have 41 pounds of pressure and somebody else says you have 38? If the pressure works, and you use the same gauge week after week, stick with it. What we really are after is performance, not a number. As for a pyrometer, it's great if you can afford one, but many racers have won and never been close to this type of instrumentation. As for track temperature, it's much the same as tire pressure. If you have a meat thermometer, and read the same instrument each week by using a known testing method, you will have an accurate comparison from track to track.

Watch for changes in the surface of a track. On an old parking lot, there will be oil and debris left from cars parking day after day. If a gate should happen to take you through such an area be aware that braking and acceleration will be decreased at that point. Look for patches in the surface. A new asphalt patch on an old lot will tend to be a little slippery when compared with the rest of the surface.

Be especially aware of short choppy dips or rises in a course. When you are running at the limit, a two inch rise or fall

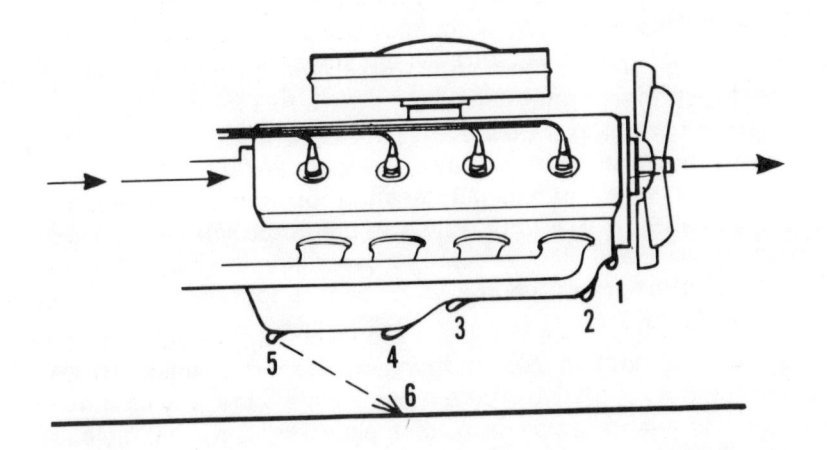

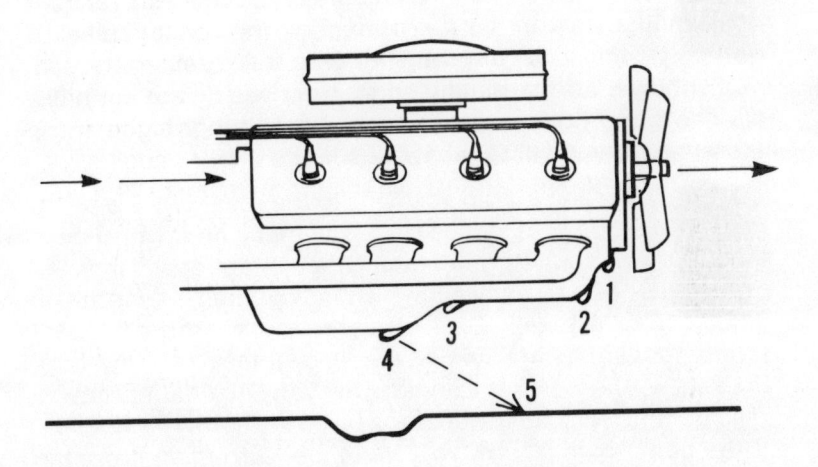

Nearly all cars drip slight amounts of oil, or other fluids. If we were to follow an oil drop, it normally starts at the front of the engine. The reason is that most connections are near the front of your engine. As a drop of fluid runs down the front of the engine, it normally ends up on the pan. The drop then travels along your pan, and is blown off the trailing edge of the engine. However, if the car hits a sudden bump, the downward force is often enough to jolt the drop loose, and it will fall to the highway.

can make a big difference in handling characteristics of your car. If you watch the surface for small shadows, you know you are coming to a surface change.

If you should run a night event, learn to read the surface with your headlights. There is a simple rule to remember that can cut winning thousandths. If the surface is falling away from your line of vision, a track will appear dark. If the surface is rising, it will appear lighter in color. The reason for this observation is that light travels in a straight line. If a surface drops, light will go over the top of a dip, thus leaving a shadow. If the surface rises, a bump will pick more light rays and appear lighter in color.

If you happen to be running a high speed event at a track, watch the road for indications of bumps. Most tracks have a discoloration from oil drops on the surface. Color and amount of oil gives us a roadmap to run by.

Nearly all cars drip slight amounts of oil, or other fluids. If we were to follow an oil drop, it normally starts at the front of an engine. The reason is that most connections are near the front of an engine. As a drop of fluid runs down the front of a block, it normally ends up on the pan. The drop travels along the pan, and is blown off the trailing edge. However, if your car hits a sudden bump, downward forces are often enough to jolt a drop loose, and it will fall to the track surface.

Let's examine a drop as it falls to the road. Since a bump made the drop fall, it stands to reason that a bump must be in front of the oil spot. By determining the average speed traveled on this part of a track, we have an idea about how far the oil landed from a bump. On a straightaway, a drop will travel farther forward before striking the road surface. In a slow turn, the spot will be closer to a bump. After you have learned how to read bumps, you can travel over a given section of track faster. If the bump is in a turn, you can either turn, then cross the bump, cross it, then turn, or compensate for additional drift you will encounter if you are turning and crossing a bump at the same time.

Try reading an oil streak in your lane on an expressway. You'll be surprised what you can learn. Watch other cars crossing the area, and watch their suspension reaction. As you cross the same spot, taking a like path, feel your car react, and compare your reaction to what you have seen. Although no two cars will react alike, you can begin to read other cars. On a track, watching other cars run can tell you a great deal about the surface.

Sideslipping and Emergency Brake Turns

There are two maneuvers in autocrossing where we do not want to be smooth. The first move we'll discuss is sideslipping.

If we look at a sample pylon layout, we'll notice that each pylon is equidistant from the next. With this type layout, we have a series of esses. Nearly every course you will ever run contains a slalom of some sort. How fast you negotiate the slalom will separate a winner from everybody else in many solo events.

Most people drive a car in and out of pylons, trying to stay close, but not hit a pylon. If we examine movement of the front and rear tracks while driving in a normal fashion, we will see the rear end tracking inside our front end. Therefore, we have to take a slightly wider arc with our front tires to keep the rear tires from hitting pylons. Exact dragover is a function of the wheelbase. If you want to know just what the distance is, pull your car into a position simulating a pylon, then measure your tracks. As a wheelbase gets longer, the dragover increases.

Let's now examine the act of sideslipping, as compared to regular driving. In order to make the car sideslip, we must 'throw' the rear end slightly, or cause our car to oversteer into a neutral position. To do this, we make two sharp, non-smooth steering inputs. First, as the driver passes a pylon (general rule — as you improve, you'll find the optimum position), turn your steering wheel sharply toward the pylon. The steering slip angle will be approximately 20 degrees. Wait approximately .4 seconds, then turn your steering wheel sharply to a zero degree, or straight ahead position. If you have made this move

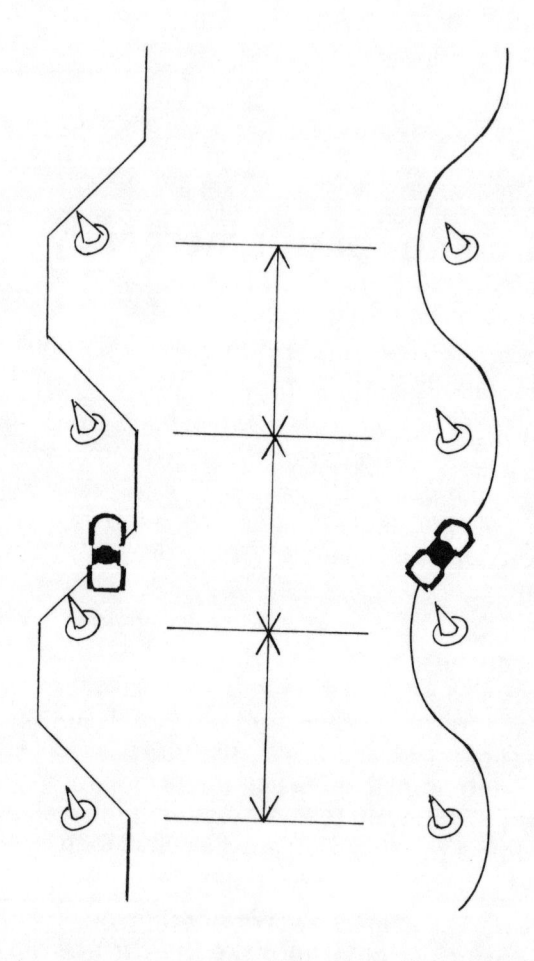

If we "throw" our car from side to side past a slalom, we can save time. This is an advanced maneuver, but once mastered will make you hard to beat. When compared to the necessary angles required to "drive" through pylons, we can see a definite advantage created by using side slipping.

correctly, your entire vehicle will move one car width in the desired direction. This is a hard move to put in writing, so don't get frustrated if it doesn't work on your first attempt. Proper speed is a function of your tires, suspension, and track surface, but once you learn the move, it can be programmed into your conditioned reflex part of the car/driver system.

A second non-smooth move is the emergency brake turn. Although we do not agree with a gimmick type autocross course (guess we're purists), there are many organizers who set up such things as courses so tight that an average driver gets down to five miles per hour or less. If you should encounter this type course, and know how to do an emergency brake turn, you might save enough time in one corner to win the whole show.

As you approach the pylons shown in gate 1, get your car spaced so you can spin 180 degrees without hitting the right side pylon in gate 1 with the rear end of your car. Slow the car with your right foot on the brake, and left foot on the clutch. As the nose of your car goes by the left side pylon, depress the clutch, and pull on your emergency brake lever. NOTE: Be sure you have your brake lever fixed so the catch is inoperative. This can be done a number of ways. On most autocross, cars, the button can be taped with 'racers tape,' more commonly known to the outside world as duct tape. On American cars, a piece of stiff garden hose can be placed behind the knob on your release lever to keep the brake from locking.

As your car starts to spin, release the brake when the rear end of your car has traveled 90 degrees, or one-half way through the turn. Let the clutch back out, and begin to accelerate through gate 2.

As with the sideslip exercise, this maneuver will take some practice, but once mastered can be a magic tool in your bag of tricks.

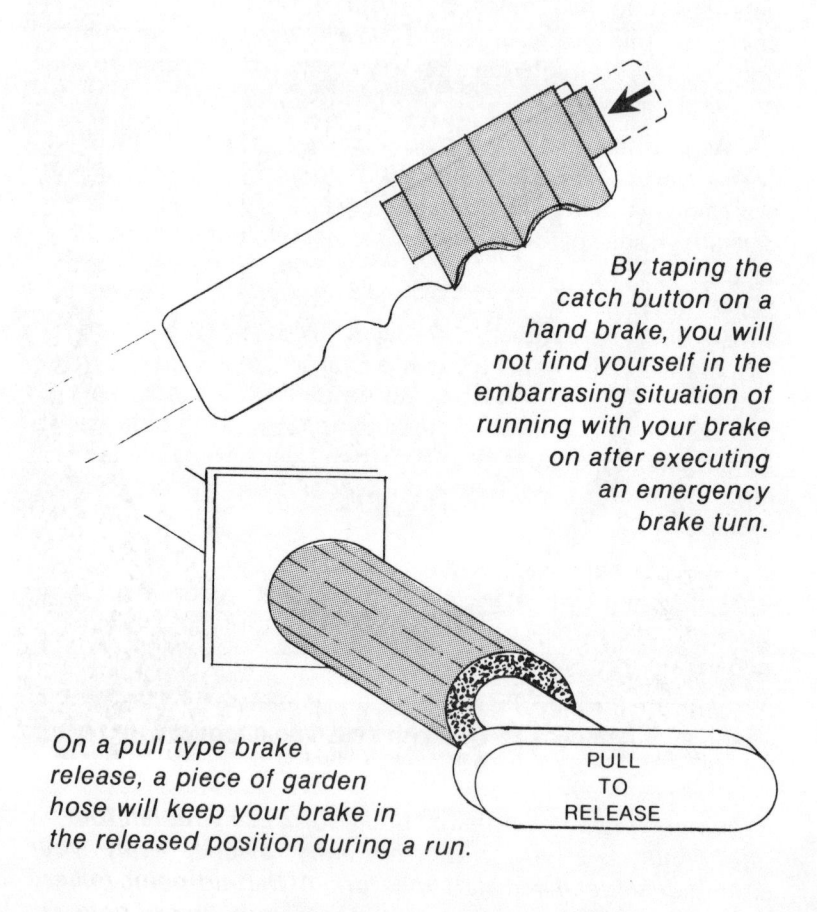

By taping the catch button on a hand brake, you will not find yourself in the embarrasing situation of running with your brake on after executing an emergency brake turn.

On a pull type brake release, a piece of garden hose will keep your brake in the released position during a run.

PULL TO RELEASE

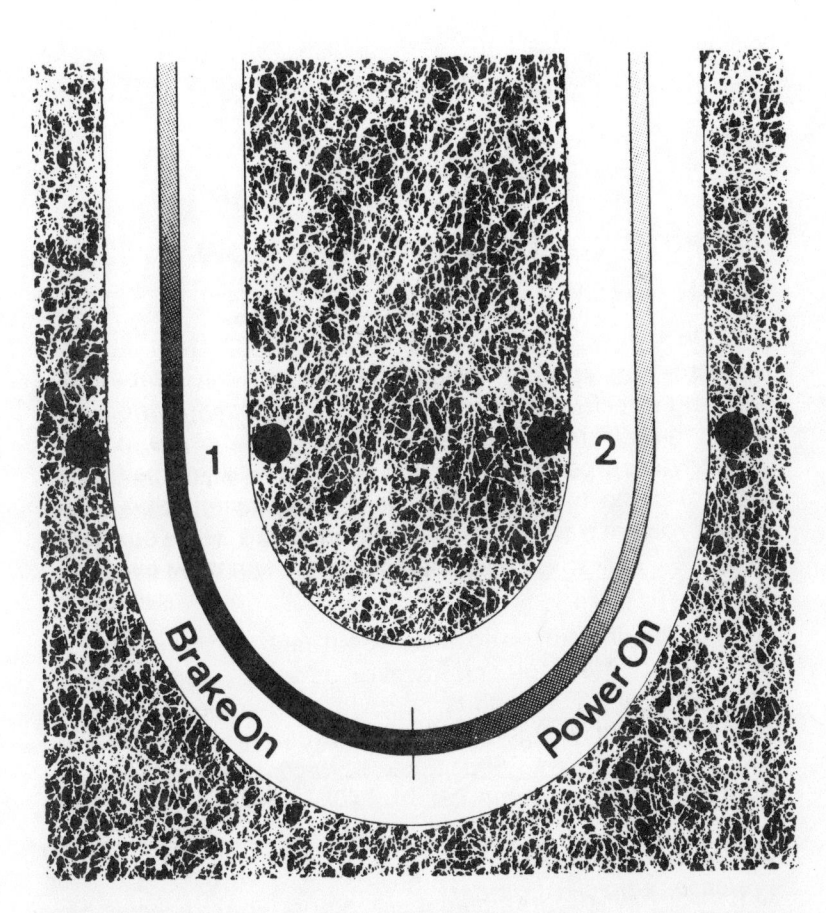

When making an emergency brake turn, use your left foot on the clutch. As you pass the entry pylons, apply your emergency brake and start your turn. At the mid-point, release your brake and begin to accelerate through the exit gate. Do not attempt to make this move at a high speed. Your exact speed will depend on the track surface, tires, car weight, etc., but will not take you long to figure out. Remember to scrub off your excess speed prior to using your emergency brake. In this instance we are using our brake as a turning assist, not a stopping feature.

Driving to the Store, or, How to Drive Your Easy Chair

Once you know the fundamentals of advanced autocrossing you can practice every time you get behind a steering wheel. What you drive is immaterial. You can practice in anything from a Ferrari to a Farmall. A corner can be read and driven properly at two miles per hour on a farm tractor. We are not being facetious; it really makes no difference what speed you are traveling. In fact, you can walk, think the proper line, then walk it. As we constantly preach, 90% of winning is mental anyway.

As you drive in traffic, think about each car you pass as the apex of a corner. You can travel on a freeway and constantly improve your driving habits. Learn to brake smoothly, with one pressure. When you get to the track, a quick mental adjustment for car, conditions, and track surface will plug in your conditioned reflex computer, and away you go.

As you start and stop in town, put an empty paper cup on the seat, or dash, and learn to drive without tipping it over. Once you have programmed these factors, you can recall them automatically, and winning becomes easier.

If we were to ask you for a quarter, you would reach into your pocket, feel the coins, and pull out a quarter. Did you look down at your pocket before putting your hand in? Did you reach in all pockets, or just one? Did you take all the coins out and visibly examine each until you saw one that stated it was worth 25¢. The answers to all questions is probably no. Why? You have been wearing pants all your life. The pockets are in approximately the same place. You most likely put your change in the same pocket, regardless of what pair of pants you have on. You have known the size of a quarter since you were a little child. As a result, you did not have to carry out many moves one might think necessary to come up with the answer to the question, "Do you have a quarter?" You have programmed your mind to know about this situation, and can handle it as a conditioned reflex. This same set of reasoning works for your driving.

How about driving your easy chair? This too can be part of a winning combination. Think about the way you will drive in a given circumstance. Run the situation through your head time after time. When you get in the street, you'll think you have been in the same place, or same type situation before — you have, but don't tell anybody it was in your living room.

Practice all the mental moves necessary to run an event. When you practice, though, don't leave out any part of the total. Think about starting your car, pulling it up to the starting line, and running the complete course. You will amaze yourself with the improvement in your driving by 'running blind.'

Transient Response

Transient response can be described as the movement across any given axis. In autocross, transient response is most often thought of as the amount of movement a tire makes traveling sideways across the rim as your car turns from left to right, or vice versa.

This thought is true, but does not encompass the totality of the term. Upon acceleration, the rise of your vehicle in the front, and the accompanying fall of the rear end is also a form of transient response. Likewise, the reverse holds true when we apply our brakes. The front end of our car dips, and the rear end rises.

Since tire movement is a most common form associated with the term, let's examine some tire builds to see what happens. The least amount of response can be found in a racing tire. Sidewalls support the tread area due to their construction, and as a result, the tread stays firmly planted under our rim. By comparison, a radial tire with low air pressure has a great deal of movement. In fact, if we were to look at a photograph of a radial tire with 24 pounds of air pressure on a heavy car, turning at a 20 degree slip angle while traveling at fifteen miles per hour, we would be shocked at how far over the rim our tire has moved.

The most practical cure for excessive transient response on a solo car is to increase air pressure. At some point, depending on the car, you will reach maximum adhesion characteristics. Going beyond this point will continue to reduce the response, but the decreased tractive ability of the tire will be more of a disadvantage than the amount of roll.

Since transient response and air pressure can affect each other, here's a little trick to measure both the tire effectiveness and the amount of tire roll due to the response rate. At four or five points around your tire, take a piece of chalk or liquid shoe polish and make a mark from the tread, down over the sidewall. Run your car with the amount of air pressure you usually use in an event. Make a number of turns, then stop and examine the chalk marks. Where chalk remains is the area not coming in contact with the road surface. If your marks come into the sidewall, add air pressure. Probably two pounds would be a reasonable place to start. Try again until you have reduced your tire roll to a point where only the area ¼ inch above your sidewall becomes scrubbed free of chalk. This should give you optimum adhesion characteristics, and reduce your transient response to a low level for your tires.

If you happen to have a set of tires with a high amount of response, but cannot afford to rush out and buy another set, learn to compensate for response by steering at a slightly different rate. As you begin to steer, be aware that your tires will pass over the center of your rim, then fall slightly as they reach the outer limits of stretch. A very slight pause in steering after your initial input will allow your car to set up in each corner without causing undo slip as your car accelerates sideways due to the response rate.

We have experimented with tires thought to be terrible autocross candidates, and found them to be quite acceptable with steering variations. This is not to say your selection should be at random, but don't feel defeated if you find a greater roll rate than you had hoped for.

Polar Moment

Polar moment can be described as the readiness with which your car can be moved away from a given direction, or path. There are three moments of inertia. They are roll, pitch, and yaw.

Roll is the movement across your vehicle. As we enter a corner, our car leans toward the outside. This is caused by centrifugal force. The word centrifugal means 'center fleeing', or the movement away from the center of a circle. As we corner, centrifugal force causes our car to attempt not to corner, thus giving a roll motion to the body. By the way, centripetal force is that force holding our car on a corner. Centripetal means 'center seeking'. As our tires are exerting centrifugal force on the road, the road is exerting centripetal force against our tires. As long as these forces are equal, we will continue to negotiate a corner. When centrifugal force exceeds the adhesion limits of our tires, we will travel at a tangent to the circle. Old Mr. Newton proves true once again.

Our second motion is pitch. Pitch is what happens as we brake sharply. Our car nose dives, or pitches. Likewise, heavy acceleration causes our nose to rise, and the rear end is forced downward.

Yaw is the moment of inertia we deal with in a spin. As our car rotates around the center of gravity, we are in a yaw mode.

All three moments of inertia travel through our center of gravity. Of the three, yaw is of most concern in a racing vehicle. Since we can live with body roll or pitch by learning to control our steering input, yaw becomes an important overall factor. Any given vehicle will only travel around a given corner at a

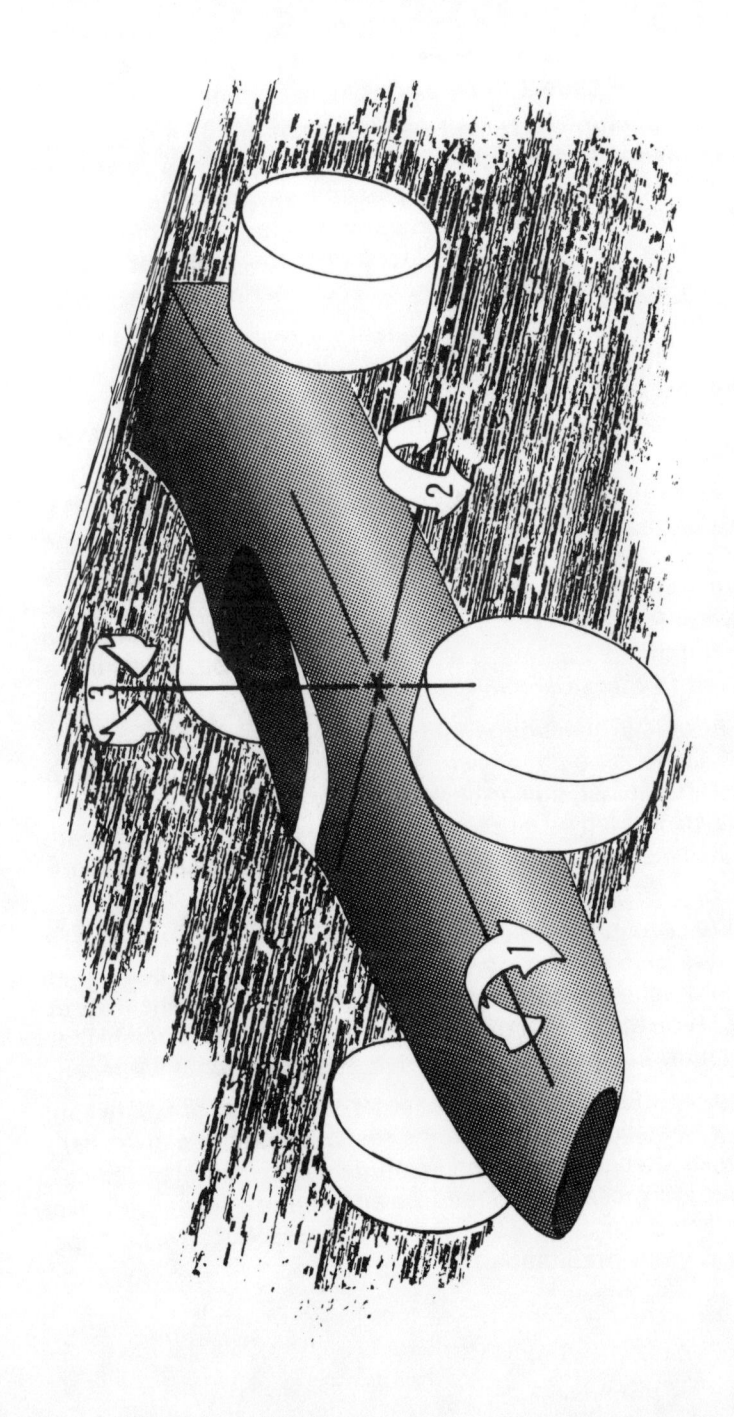

Roll (1), pitch (2), and yaw (3) all originate, and pass through the center of gravity.

given speed, on a given set of tires and suspension components. As a result, we must build yaw tolerances into our car if we expect to be a consistent winner.

By definition, a car with a high polar moment is one that will not be deflected from its path easily. In such a set up, the control factors are effectively placed away from the center of gravity. On the other hand, a car with a low polar moment is one where the masses are placed near the center of gravity, and therefore will respond quickly to steering inputs.

A car with a high polar moment will resist spinning longer, but once in a spin, will require more stopping than a car with a lower moment. However, a car with a low polar moment will start to spin more quickly, but is easier to bring back under control.

As examples, let's analyze a Pantera and a Porsche 911. The Pantera has a low polar moment due to a mid engine configuration. It will slide quicker, but is readily brought back into line by a qualified driver. On the other side of the coin we find our Porsche. The 911 will resist a change in direction longer than our Pantera, but once in a yaw motion, it is far more difficult to bring back into shape.

A logical question would be, "What is best for a Solo II car?" There is no pat answer. In reality, most cars of a certain type run against similar cars, thus any characteristics of the breed are shared by all competitors. We personally prefer cars with a lower polar moment since it is our belief they are more fun to drive.

We certainly are not knocking Porsches. They happen to be a fine piece of design and production. It is our belief that good Porsche drivers are hard to beat due to their sensitivity in a car. If you have never driven one, you may not appreciate that statement, but the Porsche purists will know what we mean.

As we mentioned in our chapter on tires, air pressure can have a tremendous effect on the response rate of a given car. Likewise, we can fake out polar moment to an extent by changing our tire pressures. In the true engineering sense, we have not affected our polar moment to any degree, but have perhaps made it more predictable.

Hydroplaning and the Autocross Car

Hydroplaning is probably one of the simplest yet least understood phenomenons in racing. To understand what hydroplaning is, we must start with an examination of a characteristic of water.

Water cannot be compressed. If you had a gallon jug of water sitting on a table, and could put the jug in a high pressure hydraulic press without breaking its container, the volume of water would not change. If we were to do a similar experiment with air, the volume would be greatly decreased. If we accept the fact that water cannot be compressed, then we must either push it out on the track surface, or run over the top of it.

A motor on a fast boat pushes on the hull until the speed is such that water can support the hull, rather than being displaced. At this point we say the boat is 'on plane'. Exactly the same thing happens to a tire. If your speed is low enough, and your car heavy enough, all tires stay in contact with the road surface. However, once the speed of your vehicle is such that water cannot escape from the tread, your front tires begin to ride up on top of the water. At this point, we are hydroplaning.

There are actually many factors that cause a car to hydroplane. The result is based on tire size, tread depth, tire pressure, weight of the vehicle, speed of the vehicle, type of surface, amount of water standing on the surface, and angle of the surface.

Steel belted radial tires are the best resistor of hydroplaning due to the integrity of the steel. The treads do not squeeze together as they do on a bias ply tire, and as a result,

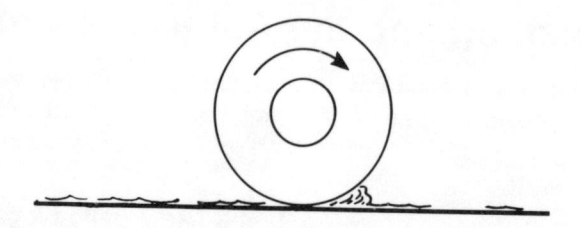

Nearly all paved surfaces become slippery the first thirty minutes after a rain starts. This is caused by oil and road dirt floating on the water. As the oil is washed off, the surface becomes more predictable. The major factor affecting a vehicle under these conditions is known as hydroplaning, or aquaplaning.

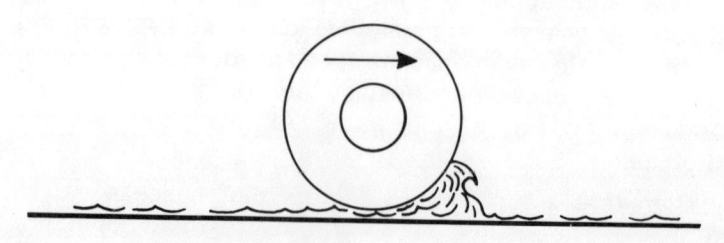

When water collects on the road surface and builds in depth, your car weight, amount and depth of tread, width of tires, speed of vehicle, etc. determines the exact speed at which your car will start to hydroplane. Water cannot be compressed, and therefore when your tires can no longer displace the water, your car rides on a cushion of water and you are hydroplaning.

grooves in the tread allow more water to be passed under the body of your tire.

If you find yourself autocrossing in rain, don't make the mistake of reducing air pressure. Many drivers feel this will improve handling, when in reality, handling ability is decreased. If you find yourself hydroplaning, there is only one move that works, slow down slightly, and don't use your brakes. Since hydroplaning is based on the fact that water cannot be compressed, compression itself can be looked on as an absolute. If this is the case, when you hydroplane, you are just slightly above the speed needed to stop hydroplaning. If you apply your brakes, all you do is close up your tire patch, and 'hydroplane better.'

Critiquing Your Performance

One of the toughest things for any of us to do is critique ourselves. First of all, if we are going to offer ourselves suggestions, then we must be able to accept the fact that we can be wrong. We run against drivers constantly who 'know' they cannot be improved upon. In fact, they'll tell you so.

At a recent autocross, Dick ran a police car as an SCCA F stock machine. He didn't intend to run at all, but it's like telling a little kid to leave candy sitting on the counter! Should have known better than to go 'watch' in the first place! The point is this. Another racer, and a good one, came up to Dick after the event and offered some constructive criticism about a given corner. He was right, and the information was both appreciated and stored in the conditioned reflex department.

By the way, the big police car ran to third place behind Tom Wright, first in a Cobra II, and a Chevy Monza, second. The Pontiac Catalina was third by less than .4 seconds. Tom was in the first advanced autocross class at NAPD.

As you complete a run, immediately review what you did. If you are a serious competitor, keep a note pad in the car, and before you get out, mark down your bad spots. Go over to the course layout sheet (if one exists), and examine the diagram. Figure out what you did wrong. If you come up with a blank, then think about the various possible causes for what happened.

Let's set the stage by saying that our car seemed to break away sharply as we approached a certain gate. The following checklist can be used for nearly any situation. Use whatever part fits your problem.

1. Lay of the track; flat, favorable bank, off camber.
2. Surface; concrete, asphalt, sand, hard dirt, other.
3. Position of the pylons with reference to the corner.
4. Tire pressure; right front, left front, right rear, left rear.
5. Tire tread; right front, left front, right rear, left rear.
6. Suspension parts; anything broken, or slipped out of place, anti-roll bar setting.
7. Steering input; turned too fast, too great an angle, not enough angle, corrected too fast, or too much.
8. Braking input; too hard, did not trail brake, changed braking rate in the corner, jabbed rather than squeezed the pedal.
9. Acceleration input; too hard, too early, too late, jabbed rather than squeezed.
10. Outside factors; oil on track, sealer at an expansion joint, or other fluid on the surface, fluid dripping on a tire from our own car, strong wind.
11. Are you driving the car, or being driven by it?
12. The last straw; if you can't get anything from the above list, forget it, the worry isn't worth the time.

Be careful about becoming SNIOPed. Don't brood. Once your run is over, and the time is in, it's over. Brooding can only bug your mind. Winners who have just lost a race still act like winners. Pseudo-winners, guys who have just overpowered the field until the real drivers came around, usually brood for weeks about it when they are beaten. Do not allow yourself to get into this category if you want to be a consistent winner.

napd CRITIQUE SHEET

CAR # _____ TYPE _____
COURSE _____
CONDITION _____
DATE _____ TIME: _____ SEQUENCE: _____

VARIABLE	UNITS	LF	RF	LR	RR
WEIGHT DIST.	lbs.				
WT. w/ ___ driver ___ fuel					
CASTER	deg.				
CAMBER	deg.				
TOE	deg. or in.				
RIDE HEIGHT	in.				
SPRING	stk.# or rate				
SHOCK	pos.#				
ANTI-ROLL BAR	pos.#				
TIRE PRESSURE	p.s.i.				
TIRE TYPE	compd.				

LAP/TIME NOTES

TIRE TEMP. DEG.

The above critique sheet will allow you to keep track of every event. You should keep a sheet on each event and each practice session. Although the contents of this book are copyrighted, we give you permission to reproduce this page in any manner you desire.

Autocrossing On Paper

Let's run a 'paper' Solo II event with first a stock Honda Civic, then the modified Pantera. The course is quite open, with fifteen foot wide gates, covering a total length of approximately 3/4 miles. The surface is concrete, and there are no limiting boundaries outside the course to crash into. The surface is level, expansion joints are narrow, and do not have excess sealer on the surface.

The starting line and stop box are set so when each car leaves, a cone is placed in what will be the stop box. After crossing the finish line, we will have 40 feet in which to come to a complete stop.

As we pull our Honda up to the starting line, we want to angle toward gate one if the starter will let us. Since we have front wheel drive, and relatively low horsepower, we do not have to worry about excessive wheel spin coming out of the starting gate.

As we come out of the gate, put the left side of our car as close as possible to the left side cone. Turn toward gate one under full power, shifting into second gear between gates 1, and 2.

As we pass gate 2, shift into third, and aim for the right side cone in gate 3. Move our car just far enough left to line up on gates 4 and 5.

As we clear gate five, brake with our left foot, and as we go past the right side cone on gate 6, move our left foot to the clutch, double clutch, and shift directly from third gear into first.

Stock Honda Civic ---
Pantera ———

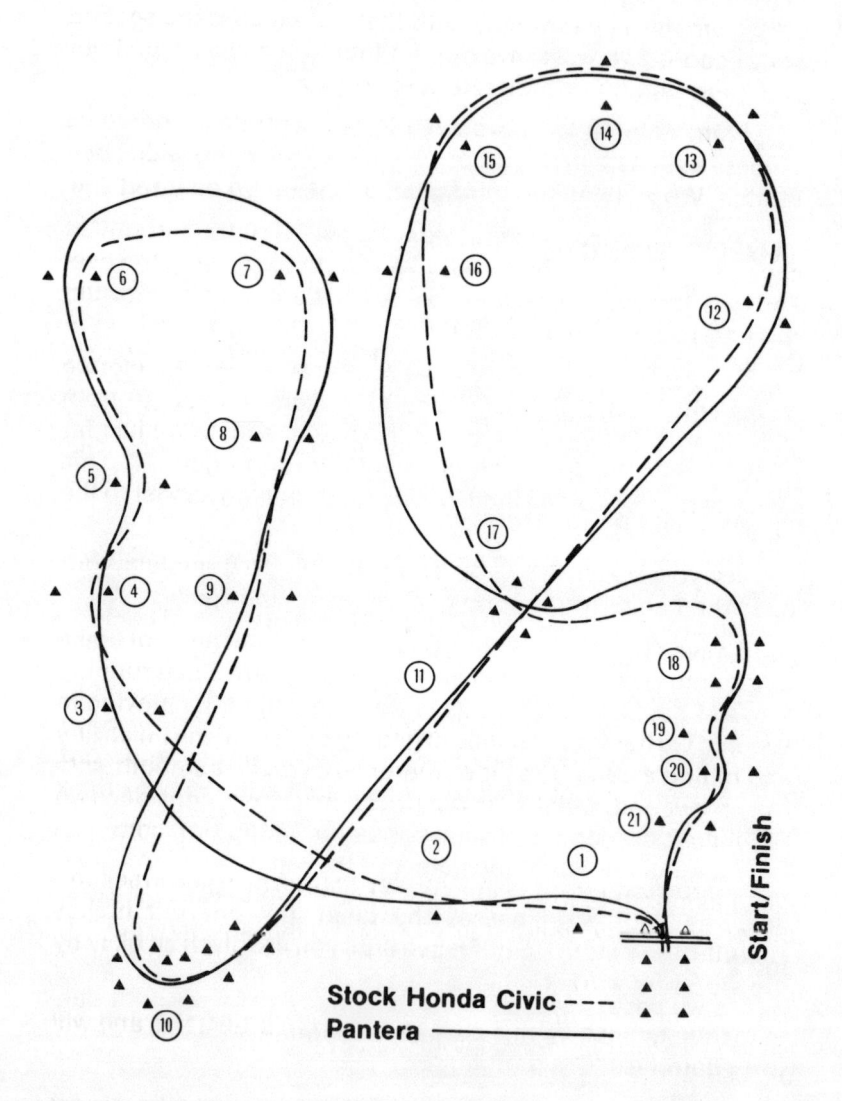

Start/Finish

106

Turn toward the right side cone on gate 7, and get on our accelerator. As we pass gate 7, we will be setting our car down, and shifting into second gear. Between gates 8 and 9 we will shift into third gear and get our little beast honking.

Gate 10 is a mistake amplifier. We need to scrub off almost 40 miles per hour of speed in order to negotiate this tricky turn. Here is where a trailing brake will really pay off. We will again shift from third gear directly into first. As we pass the second set of cones. we will move our left foot to the clutch, pull our shift, and begin to accelerate toward gate 11.

From gate 10 to 12 we need to concentrate on going as straight as possible. Do not let our car wander in this wide open stretch. We will get into third gear, and wind up near red line.

As we approach gate 12, we will brake slightly, and shift to second. In this turn, brake with your right foot, using the heel and toe method. (Reason: we will require only medium braking to pull a downshift.)

From gates 12 to 15 we have a neutral corner. Accelerate to maximum smooth speed, and stay there. As you go from gate 15 to 16, start back up to third gear speed. Move just far enough right to get a smooth sweep through gate 17. This move can be accomplished in third gear, pulling almost to the gate.

As you reach the gate, brake slightly to complete your turn, then shift into second gear by matching rpm's.

Leave your car in second gear, and use your left foot brake going into gate 18. We will stay in second here since running through gates 19, 20, and 21 is extremely tight. By staying in second, we have less chance of getting excited at the finish line and hitting a cone. The time difference between a smooth, safe run in second weighs in our favor when we consider two seconds for a cone, or five seconds for a stop box cone.

Keep your power on all the way to the finish line in second gear. As your nose passes the timer, get on your brakes smoothly and stop. Do not move until you are given an okay by the stop box worker.

Your run has been a success. You ran a 1:04.120, and will win your class. Congratulations.

Now, let's pull our Pantera up to the starting line. As you hit the switch, 550 horses scream behind your helmet. The sound will soon be so great in your car that the tach is your only true indicator of what is happening.

As you pull into the gate, angle as with the Honda. When leaving the gate, keep the rev's up to about 2500, and slip your clutch coming out of the starting box.

As your clutch catches, settle the car down and squeeze your accelerator. We pass gate number 2 under extreme acceleration, and catch second gear. We have to swing wider than in the Honda, because we are still very capable of getting excessive wheel spin if we were to jerk the steering wheel. By swinging wider, we can keep our power on.

We are now pulling in a smooth arc close to the left side cone in gate 3. By moving sharply left, then right, we can side slip gates 4 and 5.

We are now at full throttle in second gear approaching gate 6. As we approach the gate, we will pass as closely to the left side cone as possible in order to get a good arc and set up a neutral drift through gate 7. Again, we will just barely miss the left side cone in gate 7 with full power on.

We now settle the car down, shift to third gear, and hang on. As we approach gate 10, we will be flying. Swing to the right side of the gate, trail your brake into the corner, then shift to second. (Reason: we have plenty of power, and lower rpm's in second gear will not cause us to lose as much time as an extra shift coming out the other side in low gear.)

As we accelerate out of gate 10, be careful not to power slide into the last cone in the right side of gate 10.

Once again, it's hang on and go to third gear. Keep your car going straight toward gate 12, just as we did in the Honda.

As we approach gate 12, use the heel and toe method of braking, and go smoothly into second gear. Match rpm's for your shift, and squeeze the accelerator through this neutral corner.

As we pull off the turn at gate 15, stay as far right in gate 16 as possible. Let your car pull in a straight line, and take advantage of 550 horsepower between gates 16 and 17.

Make a fairly wide sweep through gate 17, and then move left. By making a wider sweep into gate 18, we can keep a higher average speed. Again, as in the Honda, stay in second gear and scoot through the remaining gates, into the stop box.

Stop smoothly after crossing the finish line. Keep your cool, you have just run a 0:54.221, and will take top time of the day.

Even though these were two 'paper' runs, your heart beat increased. If you don't believe us, get a friend to participate in an experiment. There is only one ground rule — the friend must not have seen this book.

Ask your friend to sit down. Put your hand on his or her wrist, look at your watch, and determine his or her pulse rate. Now, give them the book and ask them to read both paper runs. Keep monitoring their heartbeat. Try this experiment as often as you like, your results will be the same.

If your heartbeat goes up without actually being in a car, what happens when the real thing is before you? See now why we have tried to slow down your body motions throughout this book?

The NAPD Home Course

Running the home course at NAPD can be a frustrating experience for any driver who takes a casual look, then decides to blow down a quick run. Our track was built to train drivers, thus it has many subtleties not found in an average course. The driving surface is asphaltic concrete, ranging from 22 to 36 feet wide, and 2875 feet long. Each corner has a different radius, and the overall layout has a design speed of 30 miles per hour. Our current overall track record for a single lap is 0:55.838 seconds, set by the Pantera. We have run faster in go-karts, but these are in a different class!

At number 1, we will be turning right, very slightly off camber, and slightly downhill. At number 2, and 3, we are making a hard right at the low grade point, and swinging uphill into number 4.

As we approach number 4, we are able to see the turn from number 4 to number 5 levels off, then drops slightly into the most dangerous 'time eater' on our course. Observation of a lack of grass next to the track at number 7 tells a tale of many spoiled runs. This turn is downhill, just a tiny bit off camber, and the shortest radius on our track.

From number 6 to number 7 we designed what we felt to be a true neutral corner. There is a maximum speed for any given car, and if you exceed the maximum, you're gone. Once you lose traction, the banking is just right to carry you off the outer edge.

As we leave number 7, we once again head up hill. Number 8 and 9 will hold well if your handling is neutral, or if you have slight oversteer. If your car has a tendency to understeer, the only salvation is to get into this turn carefully, then squeeze your way through with careful acceleration.

At number 10, the track is banked slightly in your favor if you choose a proper line, but severely off camber if you go past the proper entry angle. If you find yourself 'over the hump', kiss a good run goodby!

As we move from number 10 to 11, the turn remains off camber, and downhill. Your car will tend to drift excessively toward the outer edge of the track. As you come through number 12, you are heading into a straightaway, and slightly up hill. At number 14, you need to get squarely on your binders. If you don't, at number 15 you will leave the track surface. However, if you get in right, you'll be set up perfectly for the esses.

At number 16, you are moving left, but have a tendency to stay too far right, since from 17 to 18, the track is dropping, and turning about 15 feet to the right. As we pass 18, and head into 19, the track again drops slightly, and this turn is almost dead flat.

From 19, there is just enough straight track to allow most cars to overaccelerate going into number 20. 20 starts a banked turn to the right. Rather than build a bank that would grab a car and throw it into the main straight, we banked it just enough to give an illusion of help! If you run too hard, you'll either plow off the upper edge, or loop your car. The bank must be run as a neutral corner, aiming your car for number 22.

From 22, you have an uphill straight that will allow small cars to reach about 40 miles per hour, whereas the bulls can run nearly 60 miles per hour.

Our final turn at number 23 provides the greatest thrill for a driver, and for the audience. As you approach number 23 you will notice this turn is dead flat with reference to the lay of the land, which gives you a very slight assist as you enter the turn. However, as you get ready to run for the finish line, effective banking is slightly against you.

What this all boils down to is a track that leaves absolutely no room for error. The beauty of our layout is that a really good driver can find the whole sport wrapped up in a one minute experience. Less skillful drivers usually gripe about their handling, tire pressures, the design of a given corner, or velocity of the wind!

Course number two should be well under way as this book hits the street. It will be used for higher speed training, having a design average of 60 miles per hour. The straightaways will be 36 feet wide, with corners averaging 45 feet. The length will be one mile, thus keeping a one minute run which can allow many cars to run in an event.

One of our advantages with respect to track design and construction is that one of our NAPD founders, B.W. Winder, has been in the paving business since 1949, and currently owns and operates a paving company. The tracks are designed by Dick, backed by ten years of racing experience, and a Ph.D. in concept design. B.W. and Dick do all dirt work personally, thus insuring that each track is exactly what is desired.

Another feature built into existing tracks, and to be incorporated into all future tracks is the highest degree of safety possible. A car can leave any of our tracks at any point without hitting items non-compatible with sheet metal, fiberglass, etc. As an example, the back side of our banked turn is designed in such a manner that a car leaving the road surface merely slides down the back side, which then levels out with plenty of stopping room.

The NAPD Home Course

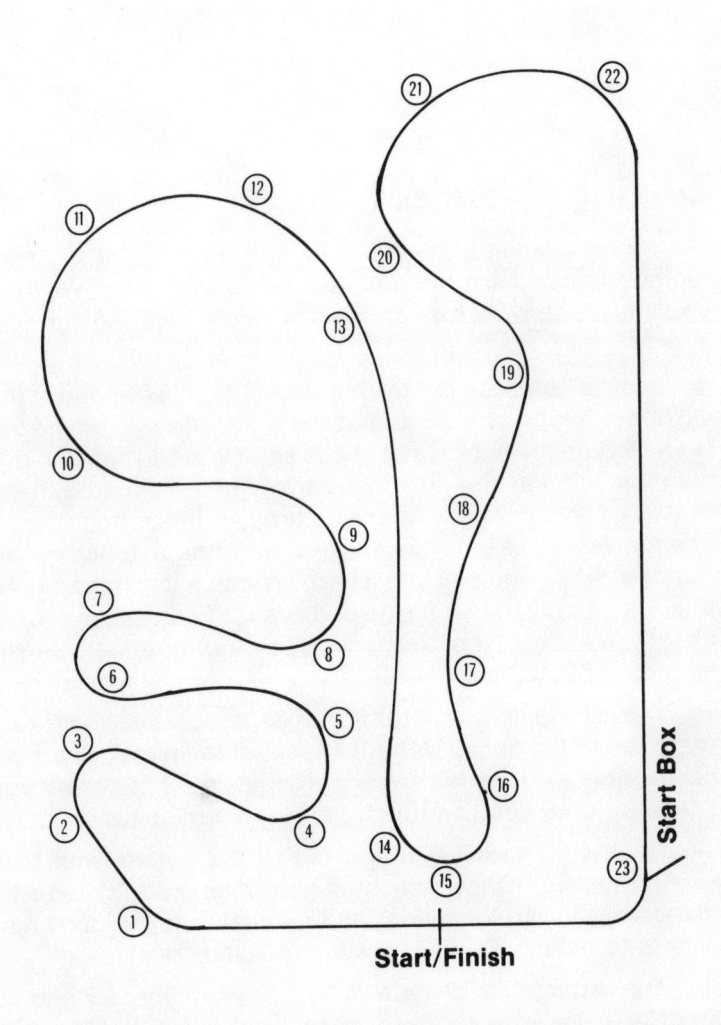

Driving Exercises

Since a small part of our driving time is actually spent racing, we can learn certain exercises to stay sharp. We'll give you a few that work for us. Use of any, or all will aid during an event.

Most drivers can put the left side of their car wherever they wish, but relatively few can put the right side tires where they wish. As you drive, pick a spot and see if you can put your right side tires on that spot. If you are traveling on a road with lane buttons, try to put your right side tires on the buttons. As you change lanes, see if you can do so without touching any buttons. When you pull into a parking space that has a painted line, watch only the right side of the lane. Try to place your car exactly in the center of the parking place without watching the left side of your vehicle.

If you have access to traffic cones, set up some cones and try to touch the cones without knocking them over. Once you can do this exercise at one or two miles per hour, work your speed up until you can touch them at event speeds.

Next, try to weave in and out of the pylons with them evenly spaced. Once you have this mastered, change the distance between the pylons and try again. (If you don't have access to pylons, do the cans full of water trick)

Try setting two or more sets of pylons just far enough apart to allow your car to squeeze through without knocking them over. Practice approaching the pylons from directly in front, and fit your car through without moving the pylons. When you have mastered this, approach the pylons from first one side, then the other.

Once you can drive through the pylons from any angle, try approaching them and sideslipping into place. When you have accomplished this move, learn to do the same thing from a sharp angle using your emergency brake.

Set up two pylons with room enough to run at them from twenty or thirty miles per hour. Learn to approach the pylons, apply your brakes with one even pressure, and stop exactly at the pylons. Once you have this move mastered, run at the pylons, apply the pressure just a little late, keep your car under control, and as you move the last two to three feet, pick your foot slightly off the brake, allowing your car to settle in a smooth stop.

Set up two or more gates in a constant radius turn. Drive your car slowly through the gate until you can feel your inside rear tire touch the inside cones. Once you have learned this move, try the same exercise at higher speed. Learn to put your car through the corner while tracking in a neutral mode. Try to negotiate your car through the corner at an even higher rate of speed. If your front end pushes, learn to scrub off just enough speed to keep from hitting pylons. If you experience oversteer, learn how to reduce your speed just enough to keep from tapping outside pylons. Another wise move would be to approach the pylons at a rate of speed you know is too high, and experience a broadslide. By going through the experience, you can learn to knock down perhaps just one pylon, instead of a bunch. In some events, you may be able to knock down a pylon and still win. This is going to be a rare occasion though, so don't count on it happening.

With the same pylon set up, practice moving your hands slowly. At first, travel at two or three miles per hour. Learn to turn your steering wheel just enough to make each corner. Now, increase the speed of your car, but not your hands. Find out how slowly you can move your hands, and still make the corner. Whatever the slowest possible steering input is, learn to do it. The slower you move your hands, the better you will balance your car.

Try lining up on an approach to a corner. Decide how much steering input will be required to have your hands end up at the three, and nine o'clock positions when you are in the turn. Move your hands to the side of the wheel as you approach the corner. By doing this, you will have a strong steering position in the corner. As you negotiate the corner, move your hands on the wheel without crossing them. You'll feel like a bus driver at first, but once you have mastered the technique, no corner will throw you. This exercise will also help to slow down your steering rate.

Practice matching rpm's as you shift while driving around town. Learn to listen to the sound of your engine at a given rpm. When you have learned the sound, take your car out of gear, set the engine on what you feel is the correct rpm, then look down at your tach.

As you learn each of these techniques, program them into the conditioned reflex department of your brain for use at the next event. Practice makes perfect, but only if the right moves are practiced.

Tips 'n' Tricks

Engine

1. Keep a separate air filter just for running events. Be sure it is spotlessly clean, and don't install it until you are at the track.

2. Indexing your spark plugs can improve combustion efficiency in your engine. Indexing is done by examining each plug, then marking the porcelain to indicate the direction of the gap. For engines where seeing the mark is impossible, file a mark on your spark plug wrench so it will line up with the mark on your plug. Place the open side, or gap, toward your intake port. This gives the most spark exposure to the charge as it enters your combustion chamber.

   If the plug will not line up properly, two changes might help. First, change plugs from one cylinder to another. If this does not work, a small spacer can be placed under the lip, thus aiding plug alignment.

3. You might wish to advance your timing slightly (2 to 5 degrees) for competition purposes. This may increase your engine temperature, but heat does not usually cause a problem in an autocross car due to the short runs.

4. You might wish to build three or four spacer blocks to fit between the base and cover of your air cleaner. The added flow may give better breathing without removing the cover completely. NOTE: This will introduce unfiltered air into your engine. If you are in a dusty situation, the risk may be greater than the payoff.

5. Higher octane ratings on gasoline mean a more even burn. To a point, higher octane fuel will increase your performance. If you are experiencing detonation, you might want to try octane additives.

6. If you are racing on an extremely hot day, you may wish to cool your fuel line with ice cubes. We have, on extreme occasions, iced the carburetor between runs. (Just the outside please!)

Suspension

7. If you are a heavy person, when you have your suspension aligned, you should either point this out to the mechanic, or have your car aligned with you sitting behind the wheel.

8. If you have a car with an adjustable suspension, remember, wedge acts diagonally, not side-to-side. By this we mean, if you jack weight into the left front, you will be loading your right rear tire. Thus, the right front, and left rear tires will lose weight.

9. If you are extremely large, you might want to wedge, or preload your suspension on the driver side to offset your weight across the car. This will give you more precise handling. However, if you are a man/wife team, one or the other of you will suffer an unbalanced car if your weight differs.

10. When driving an off-camber turn, remember, this condition will tend to make your car understeer; compensate slightly in your steering action. Likewise, a banked turn will tend to make your car oversteer.

11. Always race with a full tank of fuel, or one that is nearly empty. If you are going to run nearly empty, make sure your fuel pickup is placed in a manner that will not allow air to enter your fuel line. A partially full tank can cause an adverse handling situation as the fuel sloshes from side-to-side.

12. Check your tire pressure before you start your first run. Even if you checked pressures before leaving home, check them again at the track. Check pressure again after each run. On a tight, short course, it is not uncommon to lose air pressure due to side loading on your tires.

13. As mentioned earlier, chalk your tires before your first run in competition. After your run, check the marks

and adjust your tire pressure for optimum bite on the track surface.

14. When reading tire temperatures under competition stress, the ideal situation (but rarely reached) is to have all tires read the same temperature after a run.

15. If you wish to minimize pressure buildup during your runs, fill your tires with nitrogen instead of air.

16. If you are using a pyrometer, insert the probe at the outside edge, center of the tread, and inside of your tread. If the center is hotter than the outside edges, you have too much air pressure. If your outside edges are hotter than the center, you need to add air. If the outside edges of your front tires are hot, you may wish to change your camber in a negative direction. If the inside edges are hot, go slightly to a more positive direction with your camber. Beware however that most autocross cars will handle better with a slight negative camber setting. (Average ¾ to 1½ degrees) Don't change your camber angle for just a few degrees of temperature.

17. Racing tires for paved surfaces require a proper rubber compound. Don't be nearly as concerned with tread patterns as you are with compound hardness. A softer compound will wear more quickly, but in general, will give better bite. We say "in general," because it is possible to go too soft on some cars. In general, the amount of optimum tire pressure will rise slightly as the compound increases in hardness.

18. If you are pushing, or understeering, air added to your front tires will help as long as you are not over the maximum limits of adhesion. You can also reduce air pressure in your rear tires and accomplish a similar reaction if you are at the limit on the front.

19. If your rear tires are loose, or your car is oversteering, adding air in the rear tires will help if you are not past the maximum limits of adhesion. Likewise, reducing air in the front tires will give a similar reaction if you are at the limit on the rear.

20. Just as you roll up to start, have a friend wipe your driven tires with a damp cloth. By doing so, loose rubber and dirt will be removed, and in the case of a high powered car, the water will boil as you leave the line, transferring heat from the surface of your tire.

This will afford a slightly better bite, and your tire will not heat quite as rapidly.

21. If a course runs sharply in a given direction you might think about running stagger in your tires. Stagger is the difference in circumference, measured in the center of your tread. A stagger of four or five inches on a large car will not adversely affect straight line performance, but will impair turning in the direction of the larger tire. Rarely is this a good trick on an autocross car. We mention this effect for those extra serious folks who want to win at all costs. A car with larger tires on the right side will tend to turn left more easily. This tactic is employed on practically every dirt track car built.

22. Sensitivity can be improved through your shoes by cutting off a portion of the sole. Cut small slits across your sole to give a better feel of the pedals. Always wear flexible, rubber soled shoes. Be sure to clean any track debris from your shoes as you enter your car.

23. Never change autocross tires from side-to-side on your car. To do so will destroy the wear set, and can drastically upset your handling.

General

24. To help balance your car and offset driver weight, you may wish to move your battery, spare tire, and other heavy items to the passenger side of your car.

25. Remove your wheel covers before running an event. Wheel flex can cause a wheel cover to fly off and hit a pylon. (Right Dee?) Also clean out your trunk, remove your spare tire and jack unless you use them for legal ballast. Be sure there is nothing inside your driving compartment that can cause a distraction during your runs.

26. Before racing, check your lug nuts and be sure they are tightened to factory specifications. This is especially true if you are running trick wheels.

27. When possible, practice with your helmet on. This will give you a better feel for the engine sounds during an event. Many drivers overrev their engine during a run because they do not hear the sound as they do when not wearing a helmet.

28. Turn your inside mirror away from your line of vision. It

can be a distraction, and by moving it out of your line of sight, you won't be tempted to "wish" a clobbered pylon back into place visually. Only that which is yet to come is of value. What might be seen in the rear view mirror is only history.

29. Be sure your seat belt is as tight as you can possibly stand it. The less body motion you have, the more closely tuned you become in the closed loop system. You can stand darned near anything for a minute if it means a trophy.

30. If you wear contact lenses, wear a pair of sunglasses that fit snugly on your face. A piece of track dirt can feel like a ton of sand under a contact. Glasses will help prevent suffering.

31. On a hot day, driving gloves can help your steering grip considerably. Be careful not to carry the gloves in a sweaty hand with the palms out. Oil from your skin will make the gloves slippery.

32. If you have a long radio antenna, tie it down before running in an event. A flopping antenna can be a safety hazard, and on a tight course, can knock over a pylon. That kind of two second penalty we can live without!

33. When leaving the starting gate, keep your rpm's high enough that you do not stall, or overload your engine. Many events are won or lost in the first ten feet.

Common Mistakes

There are certain mistakes that we find in many drivers. Most of these are little things that can make a winning difference when plugged into your normal style of driving. If you find yourself represented in this list, be aware of the mistake every time you drive, and soon you will eliminate the errors of your ways.

1. Sit up in the seat, don't slouch.
2. If you are a male/female team in the same car, be sure the seat has been adjusted to your position before starting your run.
3. Be sure you have fastened your seat belt before approaching the starting line. A hastily fastened belt can cause a poor run!
4. Squeeze the pedals, don't punch.
5. Don't over-drive the course. Slow down and you will go faster.
6. Don't let time psyche you out. Forget the time, just do the best you know how.
7. If you are running a course with a stop box, shut down the instant the nose of your car passes the timer.
8. Don't make unnecessary shifts.
9. If possible, a few minutes before your run, elevate your feet. Your feel will improve, and your legs will not feel as tired. Avoid standing for long periods of time between runs. Take a folding chair, and relax!

10. Don't expect to party all night, then run a winning time the next day.

11. If you hit a pylon or have a bad corner forget it and go on. Trying to run extra hard on the rest of your run can be disasterous.

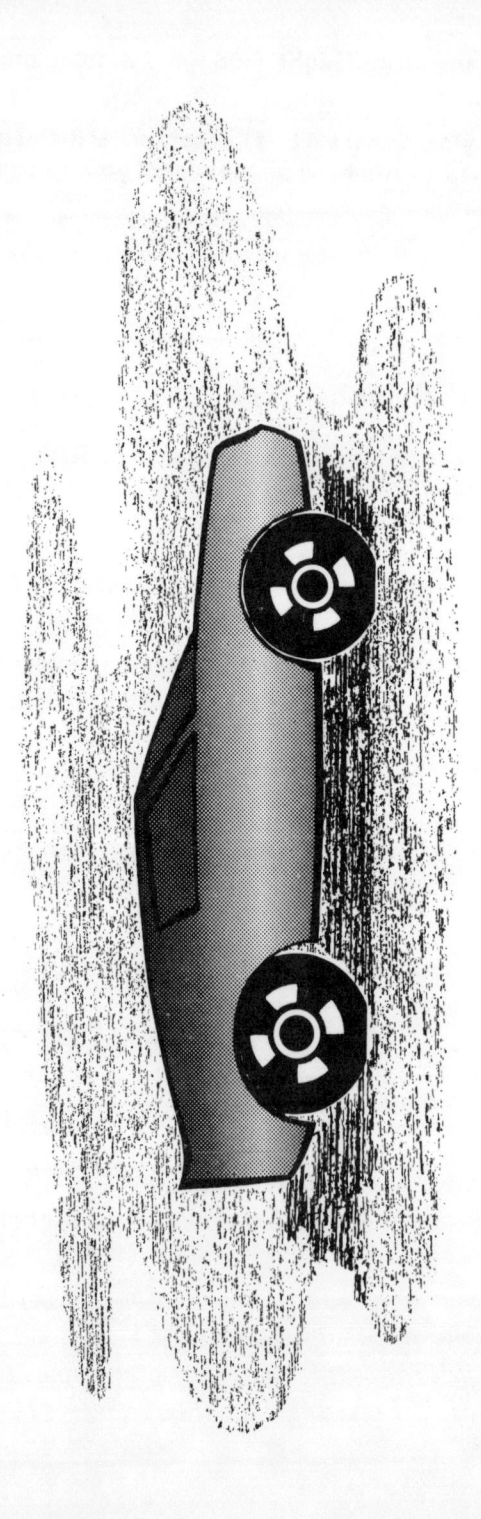

Performance driving has always held a certain mystique — herein lie the keys to driving at speed.

— Dave Shelton

Glossary of Terms

Acceleration—The addition of speed, normally caused by an engine pulling a car.

Aerodynamics—The science dealing with a race car passing through the air.

Apex—The center point of a turn with respect to entering and exiting.

Camber angle—The angle between two lines, one drawn perpendicular to the ground, and one drawn through the center of the tire.

Castor angle—The angle measured in degrees, between a line drawn through the kingpin, top and bottom bearings and a vertical line through the wheel center.

Center of gravity—The origin point of roll, pitch, or yaw. The center point at which the vehicle will balance.

Centrifugal force—The force toward the outside of a circle.

Centripetal force—The force toward the center of a circle.

Chassis set—The placement of the chassis on all four corners as measured under cornering stress, or when wedged.

Chassis stiffening—The act of adding to a chassis in order to reduce the effects of torque on the various parts.

Compression—Pressing together, caused by a squeezing from two directions, or from one direction while being resisted from another direction.

Cornering—Driving in an arc predetermined by either a limiting barrier such as a pylon, or by mental design on the part of the driver.

Dampener—A term used to describe the action of a shock absorber. A device to minimize vibration.

Deceleration—The slowing of a vehicle, normally done by applying braking pressure.

Dive—A word sometimes used to describe the pitch motion in a race car under braking.

Egress corner—A corner that exists onto a straightaway.

Emergency brake turn—A turn made with the emergency brake. This type turn is used when severe oversteer is needed.

Entry angle—The position of a car relative to an approaching corner.

Esses—A series of turns in the shape of an S.

Exit angle—The position of a car relative to leaving a corner, and approaching a straightaway.

Flog—What some folks do to a race car. To thrash, or beat a car.

G-Load—Gravity load. Normally used to describe side loading on tires. A high g means the car has good adhesion characteristics. One g would be an amount of force equal to the weight of the vehicle applied laterally across the center of gravity.

Heel and Toe—A driving method whereby the right foot is used to control both the accelerator and the brake.

Ingress corner—A corner at the end of a straightaway.

Jerk—A rapid steering motion causing an extreme overload on the suspension.

Kinetic energy—Energy in motion.

Left foot braking—Using the left foot to operate the brakes in an autocross car, thereby maintaining chassis set.

Loose—Another term used to describe oversteer.

Momentum—The impetus in a body, the force with which a car moves.

Negative camber—A situation where the front wheel leans away from the car at the road level.

Negative tracking—A state of cornering where the rear track is outside the front track.

Neutral corner—A corner with a continuous arc of more than 160 degrees.

Neutral tracking—A state where the front and rear wheels run in the same track.

Oversteer—A condition where the rear end of the car tends to come around, causing an arc greater than desired.

Pitch—A moment of inertia whereby the movement through the center of gravity is along the longiudinal axis of the car.

Polar moment—The readiness with which the car can be moved, or deflected from its path of travel.

Positive tracking—A state where the rear tracks drag over, or inside the front tracks.

Potential Energy—Energy at rest.

Precession—A gyroscopic state where the polar axis tends to deflect at 90 degrees to the direction of the applied force in a rotating mass.

Push—A condition where the front wheels scrub rather than track properly around an arc. Another word used to describe understeer.

Pylon—Those critters we try not to hit when autocrossing.

Pyrometer—A technical instrument used to accurately gauge the temperature of the rubber compound on a tire.

Roll—A moment of inertia whereby the movement through the center of gravity is along the lateral axis of the car.

Roll bar—More correctly called an anti-roll bar, this device reduces body roll and is normally mounted laterally at the front and rear of the car.

Roll center—The center of a circular arc or series of arcs as produced under the influence of a lateral force.

Rotational inertia—A rotating object tends to remain rotating about its axis.

Shock absorber—A dampening device used in conjunction with springs to reduce bounce, and stabilize the ride of a vehicle.

Spin point—The point around which a given vehicle will spin upon loss of traction.

Springs—Devices of various shapes that support the weight of a vehicle in a resilient fashion.

Stagger—Using different diameter tires opposite each other to cause the car to turn easier in the direction of the smaller tires.

Torsion bars—A supporting device much like a spring, only instead of moving up and down, they torque, or twist.

Trailing accelerator—A condition whereby the driver maintains a lag in acceleration while beginning to apply the brakes.

Trailing brake—A condition whereby the driver maintains a lag in braking while cornering, then accelerating.

Transient response—The movement across any given axis, normally referred to in autocrossing as the movement of a tire across the rim while cornering.

Understeer—A condition where the vehicle travels in an arc less than desired. The condition is also called pushing, since the front wheels push, rather than track properly around an arc.

Vector—A line of force showing the compromise result of two tractive or accelerative forces. Also the resultant force from tractive and decelerative forces.

Yaw—A moment of inertia whereby movement is around the center of gravity in a circle.

Z—Zee end of the book. Hope you enjoyed it!